T0248357

Additional praise for *The Art of Encouragement*

"If you want to become a better spouse, parent, friend, or colleague, *The Art of Encouragement* is a must read. This book includes timeless principles and practical tips for leading in all areas of life."

— Brandon Scherff,
5x All-Pro Offensive Lineman with Jacksonville Jaguars

"Jordan's vulnerability in sharing personal stories from some of the hardest times in his life lends this book an undeniable authenticity. He beautifully illustrates the transformative power of genuine encouragement and selfless service to others, guiding readers toward fostering meaningful connections with those around them."

— Tyler Shatley,
Offensive Lineman, Jacksonville Jaguars,
franchise record holder for games played

"Jordan has an unparalleled ability to lead and communicate. He brings infectious energy to every interaction and environment. *The Art of Encouragement* allows readers to learn from one of the top encouragers on the planet and put Jordan's unique principles into action."

— Fran McCaffery,
Head Coach, Iowa Men's Basketball

"At a time when so many are looking to tear others down, I have never met anyone so anxious TO LIFT PEOPLE UP! Jordan is the very definition of someone who leads from the front and does so enthusiastically, authentically, and every single day. *The Art of Encouragement* is the right book at the right time and an absolute must-read!"

— Jim Rome,
Top American radio personality and
host of the award-winning *Jim Rome Show*

"Jordan has been extremely impactful in my development not only as an athlete, but a man as well. I'm thankful for his friendship and mentorship!"

— Trey Smith,
Offensive Lineman and 2x Super Bowl Champion,
Kansas City Chiefs

THE ART OF ENCOUR AGE MENT

HOW TO **LEAD TEAMS**, **SPREAD LOVE**, AND **SERVE FROM THE HEART**

JORDAN MONTGOMERY

WILEY

Published by John Wiley & Sons, Inc., Hoboken, New Jersey.
Published simultaneously in Canada.

For general information on our other products and services or for technical support, please contact our Customer Care Department within the United States at (800) 762-2974, outside the United States at (317) 572-3993 or fax (317) 572-4002.

Wiley also publishes its books in a variety of electronic formats. Some content that appears in print may not be available in electronic formats. For more information about Wiley products, visit our website at www.wiley.com.

Library of Congress Cataloging-in-Publication Data:

Names: Montgomery, Jordan (Writer on Encouragement), author.
Title: The art of encouragement : how to lead teams, spread love, and serve from the heart / Jordan Montgomery.
Description: Hoboken, New Jersey : Wiley, [2024] | Includes index.
Identifiers: LCCN 2024011188 (print) | LCCN 2024011189 (ebook) | ISBN 9781394234479 (hardback) | ISBN 9781394234554 (adobe pdf) | ISBN 9781394234486 (epub)
Subjects: LCSH: Encouragement. | Leadership.
Classification: LCC BF637.E53 M66 2024 (print) | LCC BF637.E53 (ebook) | DDC 158.3—dc23/eng/20240424
LC record available at https://lccn.loc.gov/2024011188
LC ebook record available at https://lccn.loc.gov/2024011189

COVER DESIGN: PAUL MCCARTHY
COVER ART: © GETTY IMAGES | CIPELLA

SKY10076425_060424

To my wife Ashley and my children, Audrey, Claire, Olivia, and Mackoy. Your love and encouragement mean everything to me.

Contents

Foreword

There have been many books written on leadership and personal growth, but there are few written by authors who genuinely live out the subject they teach. At this stage in my life, I'm looking to learn from leaders whose lives match the lessons they share with others. That's why I couldn't wait to read this book. Jordan Montgomery is one of the greatest encouragers I've ever known.

You've heard it said, encouragement is oxygen for the soul. I'll never forget my father asking me, "John, do you know how I know if someone needs to be encouraged?" After a brief pause, he answered his own question, "If they're breathing!" In other words, everyone needs to be encouraged. That's why every leader needs to read *The Art of Encouragement*.

As a mentor and friend of Jordan, I've had the privilege of observing his leadership journey and witnessing his commitment to personal growth. Jordan is not content with merely navigating life. He is constantly seeking wisdom by asking profound and thoughtful questions to better himself and those around him. His curious spirit propels him forward, and he embraces every opportunity to expand his impact on the world.

The Art of Encouragement is a timely message for any leader. We are living in a world where negativity gets the headlines, and division has become the norm. I see too many leaders doing whatever it takes to win, even if it's at the expense of others. This type of leadership is self-centered and destined to fail. The truth is self-centeredness and leadership are incompatible. You cannot be all about yourself and lead well at the same time. Because leadership is all about others.

As a motivational speaker and coach, Jordan has integrated the principles of encouragement into his work, leaving an unforgettable impact on everyone around him. He is one of the most well-connected young leaders I know. Why? Because his influence shines with optimism and belief in others.

In the book, Jordan teaches 10 "arts" of encouragement, each revealing his sincere goal of empowering others to better their lives and the lives of those around them. He and I share this desire—that you would be gripped by the reality that there is transformative power in uplifting words. And that you would apply these timeless lessons to your life.

I believe this book will serve as a catalyst for the positive change Jordan is destined to bring to the world. He embodies the spirit of encouragement, and as you navigate the pages of *The Art of Encouragement*, you'll find yourself in the capable hands of a guide who not only talks the talk but walks the walk.

—John C. Maxwell

Acknowledgments

I want to give a very special "thank you" to John Maxwell, Mark Cole, Chad Johnson, Jared Cagle, and the entire Maxwell Leadership team. It's an honor to have the Maxwell Leadership stamp on this book. Your unwavering support and belief in my work has made this book possible. I am eternally grateful for your guidance and friendship. I want to also extend my deepest appreciation to Elanie Welch. I am forever grateful for your support and contribution to this book. Thank you also to the Wiley Publishing team for helping to get this message out into the world. Your support has been wonderful!

Introduction

A note: Out of respect for the individuals involved, some names, facts, quotes, associations, companies, and identifying details have been changed in order to protect anonymity and keep privacy intact. Quotes have also been approximated to the best of my memory, or paraphrased for narrative flow.

As a performance coach, I have had the privilege of coaching people from various backgrounds and walks of life, people who are involved in different industries and who are from different parts of the world. As you might expect, these individuals have different personalities with very different worldviews and belief systems. It has been a tremendous honor to do this work, but with it comes a deep sense of responsibility. I must be very thoughtful about how I choose to engage with the people I coach; as in any relationship, establishing trust is paramount, and this requires me to show that I see and understand each client as a unique person. I must give a great deal of consideration to their individual traits and characteristics, taking into account their background and life experience. I must understand and match their communication style, and in a matter of minutes, create a meaningful connection. These individuals are placing their trust in me as a coach and will share with me the intimate details of their life—oftentimes, in our very first conversation.

I have learned that every client is different. Some people want me to simply listen, and others almost immediately ask for advice. Some show up with detailed agendas while others prefer an open framework for discussion. Some are more skeptical while others are more trusting. While each conversation with each new coaching client is unique, I have learned that one thing is true with all of these people and in every interaction. They all understand one language: the language of encouragement. They all want to feel seen, heard, and understood. They want to be appreciated and acknowledged. Encouragement is a universal language heard and understood around the world. Everyone loves to hear it spoken, and not enough people are speaking it.

In this book, my hope is that you will discover some new truths about the language of encouragement, a language that you may already be familiar with. While encouragement is a simple topic, it isn't something that we should dismiss or take lightly. It is also not a tool to be wielded for manipulation, used for getting what you want out of people or from people. The purpose of this book is to help you apply the Art of Encouragement so that you can lead, love, and serve from the heart.

As you begin to dive into this book, I invite you to ask yourself some reflective questions on the topic of encouragement—how well are you doing at encouraging your spouse, your children, or your coworkers? Most likely, if you are being honest with yourself, you will admit that your ability to encourage others needs a little work. Nobody is perfect. In full transparency,

I myself have a great deal of work to do in learning to be a better encourager, and I wrote a book about it! We often struggle with putting what we know into practice. It seems there is a gap between knowing and doing as it relates to this topic. In other words, most people know that encouragement matters, but few people put it into action intentionally and consistently. Common sense isn't always common practice.

For the last several years I have engaged in an onboarding exercise with new coaching clients in our executive coaching practice. Most of these individuals have had at least some level of success, whether in business, sports, or life in general. As part of our discovery work, we ask new clients to supply us with contact information for two people who know them well: one person who knows them well personally, and one person who knows them well professionally. I want to get to know our client through the eyes of the people who know them the best. This type of exercise and debrief is typically very encouraging. They get the opportunity to hear from their spouse, best friend, significant other, etc. about their strengths, abilities, and opportunities for growth.

Once I have acquired the responses to the questions, I bring them to my client. I set the table, letting them know that they don't have to do anything with this information, they simply get to receive it and allow themselves to be encouraged by it. I am sure to read the responses slowly, as I want the words to truly resonate with my client.

As we finish the exercise, I always ask the same question: "So, how does that make you feel?" And almost every single time there is an emotional response. I hear comments like "Wow, that just means so much to me" or "I am so fortunate to have them in my life." Sometimes there is just silence after I ask that question as my clients attempt to collect themselves. It is a fun and unique moment to share with them; they have just been tremendously encouraged by someone they care deeply about!

What I find so interesting about this practice is how incredibly impactful it is, despite its inherent simplicity. It takes roughly 15 minutes to complete the full exercise, from sending the questions to receiving the responses and sharing them. I ask five very basic questions about strengths and growth opportunities: "what do you admire most about John?", "what are John's greatest strengths?", "what does your relationship with John mean to you?", etc. This person gets to hear from someone they know very well, but because we took the time to extract true feelings that might not be easily shared otherwise, we create a very unique and special experience. We assume the people in our lives know how we feel about them, that they know how great we think they are—but this is not usually true! It serves as great evidence and proof that people aren't encouraged as much as they should be or could be.

In the pages that you are about to read, I will share some of my own personal experiences and use those experiences to demonstrate the Art of Encouragement. The principles are basic; the application of the principles is not. Often the simplest principles are the most difficult to apply, but fear not, I've given you a way—read on!

Reader Challenge

To help you actually *do* something with the information you learn in each chapter, we have created a fun and meaningful challenge that we think you will find to be an impactful opportunity. At the end of Chapter 1, you are asked to write down the names of 10 individuals in your life, whether it's a coworker, your spouse, a family member, a friend, your mailman, or the check-out person at the grocery store. For the next 21 days (or however long it takes you to read this book), you are going to actively work to encourage these individuals using each of the principles you learn here. Each subsequent chapter has its own unique exercise to try out. If you really take the time to do these exercises, and do them intentionally, I promise you will see life-changing results.

The language of encouragement is universal. Everyone can speak it, everyone can understand it, and everyone needs it. The average person underestimates the power of encouragement. But you, dear reader, are about to see just how incredibly powerful it can be.

Are you ready? Let's dig into the Art of Encouragement!

Chapter 1

The Art of Uplifting Encouragement

My early twenties found me like most new college graduates—optimistic, well-educated, and completely aimless. All through my high school and college years I worked numerous odd jobs—from selling gym memberships to delivering furniture to driving a garbage truck. (I told my friends I worked in "waste management," which sounded much nicer than "I sort people's trash.") I eventually moved from throwing away people's stuff to selling people stuff, and after some years of various sales jobs, I landed a position as a financial advisor in the financial services industry, in a Fortune 100 firm with a branch office located in Iowa City, Iowa.

I quickly grew to love this new career. I enjoyed building relationships and the work itself was fulfilling. I started putting in long hours, showing up early and leaving late. I was eager to learn and loved seeking advice from those in the profession who had come before me.

Soon, my career became my identity. I woke up thinking about it, and I went to bed with it still on my mind. I began receiving awards and recognition, which motivated me further and fueled my drive. I was proud of my accomplishments in this new and exciting career. After a few years, I was promoted to a managerial role. At that time, I was the youngest person to be given such a high-level leadership role at the firm. I was sure this was the place for me—I had found my calling. I was young, deeply motivated, and energetic—intent on investing everything I had into building the illustrious future I knew would continue to flourish and grow.

Until the day that everything changed.

Have you ever heard the term "valley season?" If you are at all familiar with valleys, you know that they are often winding, unpredictable, ever-changing, and hard to see your way out of—much like the aptly named "valley seasons" of life. A valley season in life often brings with it a long, low emotional expanse between high points. A season that young, naïve me was about to enter.

The Beginning of the End—My Slow Descent into the Valley

It began with a text from my supervisor.

We'll call him Steve.

"I need to speak with you right away. It's very important, and I'm requesting you come in to my office at 8 o'clock tomorrow morning."

You might think that my first reaction would have been to be terrified, but actually, I was more annoyed than anything (told you I was naïve). I was pretty busy with my work, and the meeting felt like an inconvenience.

I picked up my phone and texted Steve back:

Hey, I've got a busy morning of meetings, I'd prefer if we meet another time, if that's alright?

The response back was immediate.

"This is the kind of meeting you need to clear your calendar for," it said. "I'll see you at 8 o'clock."

My brain went into hyper drive. What could this be about? I didn't really think it could be about something I did. Maybe someone on my team had made a mistake? Yeah, that had to be it. Someone *else* had totally screwed up. Right?

Okay, so maybe I *was* a little bit terrified. I began revisiting every detail of my last several days, every little interaction I had, things I said, people I saw. Did I do something, and I wasn't aware of it? Was it something I said?

I felt sick.

Worst-case scenarios were coursing through my head. I knew exactly what I needed in that moment.

I took my phone out and called my dad.

My dad is a man of deep faith. He radiates a wisdom rooted in his wonderful, unshakable belief that God is always in control. It is a key part of his strength and tenacity and one of the reasons I have come to depend on him so much, especially in the hard moments.

"Hey Dad," I said, and hardly able to contain myself, I started right in without giving him a chance to even say hi back.

"I got this really bizarre text from Steve, and it's super concerning and I can't really talk to him about it until tomorrow morning and I'm just totally stressed out and worrying—maybe people are upset with me?"

The Art of Uplifting Encouragement

I continued to ramble. My father listened patiently. After some time, I stopped, waiting for his response.

He started, and then paused.

"I'm sorry son," he said, finally, seeming to weigh every word carefully. "That seems hard, and unfair . . . but maybe God's trying to teach you something."

Not exactly what I wanted to hear at the moment. He pressed on.

"You're healthy," he said. "You have a lot of great people around you. You have a lot of reasons to be joyful and optimistic. Let's pray."

And so, together we prayed. The day before one of the hardest days of my life, the day before everything I had—everything I knew myself to be—would crumble, the day before I experienced repercussions that would change the course of my life—I prayed with my father.

"God, we trust you, *we trust you. . .*"

But I continued to worry.

The Valley Floor—aka Rock Bottom

The next day, after a restless night, I woke up still feeling sick to my stomach. I called my dad again to check in, and we prayed together one more time.

God has a plan, I told myself.

I know there is a plan.

And this will all be okay.

. . . right?

My morning commute felt like a thousand miles, each mile stretching further and further, as though I was driving on a treadmill instead of a highway.

I walked in to the office with heavy feet and a stomach swimming with dread, and was greeted by Tracy, a familiar face.

"Hi Jordan," she said, dryly. "Can I get you some coffee?"

Coffee.

It hardly registered. She might as well have been offering to fill my briefcase with chili, for all I noticed. All I could think about was how different she seemed. Normally, we would talk about life, chat about things going on in the office, maybe make a friendly joke. But not today.

Today was different. It was tangible.

The two excruciating minutes I spent in that lobby were the longest two minutes of my life. It felt like I was sitting there for years. Suddenly the seat I was in was uncomfortable. My senses were on overdrive. It was hot, and stuffy, and it smelled like leather. A fly was buzzing, hitting the window. *Bzz, bzz, bzz, tap, tap, tap.*

Steve walked into the lobby.

He's lean, confident. He has a sense of understated power.

Usually, he'd say something dry and sarcastic. But there is only:

"Hey, Jordan."

I looked at him, he and Tracy like statues, and I felt like I had shown up to a party where everyone was invited and knew what was going on, except for me.

He gestured toward the door, and I walked into a little side conference room, with four chairs around a small rectangular table. The blinds were drawn—*why are the blinds drawn?*—and I was sure the thermostat must have been set to 90. There were harvest landscape paintings. Dim lighting. Everything was meant to be warm, inviting, homey, but instead it just felt dark, dusty, suffocating.

We sat down, and Steve turned to face me.

His face was rigid and unsmiling. "I'm sorry, Jordan," he began. "But I need to warn you now, this is going to be pretty uncomfortable for you."

My heart was nearly pounding out of my chest. *Thump thump, thump thump, thump thump.*

For the first time, I noticed a large folder sitting on the table. Steve opened it.

It felt like a police investigation.

An incredibly thorough police investigation.

The folder was full of documents.

Text messages.

Emails.

Receipts.

All put together, printed out, and—

I wasn't prepared for this. I wasn't prepared for any of it. I was now visibly sweating, *why is it so hot in here?*

The room started to spin.

"Jordan," my name sounded caustic coming out of his mouth. "Where were you when you completed this assessment on December 9th?"

My tongue felt swollen. My mouth dry. My palms sweaty.

I tried to speak, and my voice croaked.

"I-I, I don't know."

My face was turning red, I could feel it.

Steve started asking more questions.

And more questions.

And more questions.

And all I could muster was "I don't know." I mean, who remembers where they were at random dates and random times?

"We track VPN logins," Steve said. "And we can tell where you logged in from. Your computer was not logged in when you took this test. We verified that someone else took this test on your behalf."

He was right. It was no use pretending otherwise.

"Yes, that happened."

Steve nodded, then glanced at me.

Tears were spilling down my face. Steve quickly looked away, shuffling through the papers.

More questions followed. More mistakes came to the surface.

I knew that in my quest to grow my career I had been careless and casual—that much was clear now.

I felt like I was dying.

It was pretty obvious what was about to happen, but I couldn't think about it. Everything I'd worked for—everything I understood about myself—the status I'd wanted, the lifestyle I worked to achieve, the money . . .

It couldn't end this way.

If I didn't have this job, if I didn't have this position, this lifestyle—my whole identity would be gone.

I couldn't even ask any questions. I felt raw. Hollow.

"You're going to be in touch with us," Steve said. "But today's your last day."

I nodded.

And that was the end of it. The end of life as I knew it.

Because of my leadership role inside the company, an email had been sent out about my termination to hundreds of people. People I knew and respected. Peers and colleagues, managers and leaders, friends and strangers.

Everyone knew.

I was humiliated, drowning in shame. I had screwed up, and it was on public display. What would they think of me? Surely, I was forever engrained in their minds as a terrible person, a failure, a tainted, stained human being.

How would I ever recover?

The Power of Uplifting Encouragement

The days blurred by. I could barely put one foot in front of the other.

One morning, my brother and his wife and I were sitting together at the kitchen table, in silence.

The fallout from the firm—all of it was around me, reverberating inside of me. I couldn't stop thinking about it. I couldn't stop feeling it. I felt sure my family must hear all the internal rattling inside of me, it was so loud.

"Dude," I said, finally. "Am I going to be okay?"

My brother looked at me, his face set and determined.

"No," he said. "You're not."

What? That wasn't what I was expecting to hear. My stomach dropped.

I didn't know what to say. My throat started burning. I looked down at my shoes, and then back up at him.

A light twinkled in his eyes.

"It's not going to be okay," he said. "Because it's going to be better than okay, it's going to be *great*."

I stared at him in disbelief. Great? How?

My sister-in-law chimed in "There is a reason you're going through this. God didn't cause it, but maybe he is allowing it."

Without hesitation, unwaveringly, my family believed in me. As we continued to talk, and they continued to share their encouraging optimism for my life, I couldn't help it, I started to believe that maybe they were right. The air seemed to shift. The fog was clearing. With just one simple conversation, my family had given me the tools I needed to begin my ascent out of the valley.

Now years later, as I tell my story, I remember what an impact those simple words of encouragement had on me.

In the valley of struggle, when things are tough—when we feel like we might be lost forever in those winding, unpredictable depths—that's when encouragement has the greatest possible impact. Just like to a starving man, a meal can be the difference between life and death, so encouragement feeds the soul of a desperate valley wanderer. The beauty of encouragement in these difficult moments of life cannot be described. Uplifting encouragement is named so because in the darkest moments of our valley seasons, it lifts us up out of the depths.

The Art of Uplifting Encouragement

I can tell you each and every word of uplifting encouragement spoken during my valley season was a lifeline to me. Even if I couldn't totally believe in it at the time, I can still vividly remember the people who called me, and exactly what they said.

Psalm 34:18 says

The LORD is close to the brokenhearted and saves those who are crushed in spirit.

For me, my spirit was crushed.

My mind was clouded with negative thoughts.

And in that season, the natural, inherent optimism and positivity I took for granted that I would always have—it just wasn't there anymore. I needed others to offer it to me. I often think back to that moment in the kitchen with my sister-in-law and my brother—their tone, their body language. Their uplifting encouragement in that moment was exactly what I needed.

That, I will never forget.

"There's an amazing plan for your life," they said.

Their hope and optimism were transferred to me, and they truly helped me shift my thinking from despair to the idea that everything really could be okay, and in fact, better than okay. That day, my family changed my life through uplifting encouragement. They demonstrated the power of encouragement wielded responsibly.

It's easy to dismiss encouragement. To view it as a "fluffy" idea, or a "nice-to-have" trait. To downplay it.

Don't do that.

Encouragement is the lifeblood of positivity and optimism. It is the foundation of teams, communities, and families. Every single person needs encouragement. Every athlete, coach, parent, professional—they all run on the idea that the future holds goodness and that no matter what happens they have what they need inside of them to deal with it.

It was through my own personal experience (and many others that I will detail in this book) that I've come to believe that encouragement is one of the most important tools any of us have at our disposal. And I want this book to be the guide, the principles, the lessons, and the catalyst for your own journey in wielding the power of encouragement.

In your workplace, in your home, in your community—it doesn't matter what title you hold. You can make an impact when you encourage.

Reader Challenge

My hope in sharing my personal story is to show you the power of the Art of Uplifting Encouragement, the type of encouragement that can bring someone out of the depths of a valley season. Uplifting encouragement is the kind that reminds someone to reflect with gratitude on all they have in light of difficult circumstances. It helps to magnify the positive in our lives, and reminds us that even our most difficult life events can work together for our good. It casts a vision for a brighter, better future.

My family members were some of my greatest encouragers during my valley season. My family provided this type of encouragement for me in a moment when I needed it the most, and I hope I can inspire you to do the same for others in your own life.

Unfortunately, we don't always have the advantage of knowing when someone is in a valley season. So often we answer the cursory "how are you?" with the expected "fine, thanks, and you?" regardless of how things are going. Very rarely do we ask that question and receive a specific and honest response.

So how can you know when someone is in a valley season and needs to be encouraged?

The answer is easy, are you ready for it?

You don't have to know.

Here's my challenge to you, dear reader:

Encourage the people in your life at least once a day, every day, regardless of how you think they are doing. If you can do this, you will naturally encourage someone wherever they are at in their journey—in their valleys, on the plains, or at the top of a mountain.

We often hear that it takes 21 days to form a new habit. So, try to implement the principles you learn within this book to encourage at least one person, at least once a day, every day, for 21 days straight.

Use this space to write down the names of 10 people you would like to encourage. It doesn't matter if it's a coworker, a spouse, a family member, a friend, your mailman, or the check-out person at the grocery store. Just write 10 names here:

1.

2.

3.

4.

5.

6.

7.

8.

9.

10.

Over the course of the next several weeks (or however long it takes you to read this book), you will learn how to encourage each of these people using the principles you learn in each chapter of this book. Take note of how your life, and the lives of the people around you change with this simple habit. Write your observations in the Observations section at the end of the book!

Chapter 2

The Art of Self-Encouragement

The War Room

The summer after my termination was a challenging season.

One evening during that time I attended a Matthew West concert with my dad, who had flown in from Iowa to visit me. The fallout from my firing was very fresh.

I studied my dad as he sang along to the worship music, appreciating him. He was a rock for me. While I had so many people offer meaningful support and guidance—my dad got the most real moments of my despair. I called him every day, and he was a constant ear to listen. We talked about God, about life, about the importance of staying steady, even in hardship.

He repeatedly pointed me back to God, reminding me to trust God and lean in to His plan for my life. He brought me back to scriptures and truth, time and time again. I'll admit, at times I was frustrated by his approach. I wanted there to be concrete answers.

How do I actually fix the mess I'm in?
What do I do?
How do I do it?

And my dad, always the steadfast, patient, and kind mentor, would continue to point me not to specific solutions but to known truths:

God does His best work in the valley.

Remember, you're learning through this.

Trust in God's plan.

He went back frequently to James 1:2-3:

"Consider it pure joy, my brothers and sisters, whenever you face trials of many kinds, because you know that the testing of your faith produces perseverance."

Pure joy over my trials? That one was hard to wrap my head around.

After the concert my dad and I were sitting in my apartment, talking and hanging out together. The weekend was drawing near the end, and my dad was going to leave. This was the part I dreaded the most.

I had moved to a different city to re-start my career and I spent so much time in that apartment alone. In my free time I was left to my own thoughts. I often felt weighed down by the burden of uncertainty about the future, and shame about the past. I frequently allowed my thoughts to wander down darker paths and found myself ruminating on the same negative mental scenarios over and over again. My dad being in town helped tamper those feelings, providing a loving distraction from my anxiety. But if he left, it felt like the dam would burst and it would all come flooding back.

"Dad . . . ," I started.

I paused—feeling myself start to well up.

"You're going to leave," I said. "We had such a great weekend. I know Monday is going to come here any second, and I'm going to be so discouraged, and I just hate that like—"

He listened patiently, while I found words.

"You're going to walk out that door," I said. "and I know the reality of my situation will hit hard when you leave."

We sat in silence for a few minutes before my dad spoke, weighing his words.

"You know, Jordan," he began, "as comforting as it is to sit and pray with me, I want to remind you that you've got a God you can sit with anytime."

He looked at me.

"Can I help you with that?" he said.

I hesitated for a moment. I didn't really know what he meant.

"Um," I said, blinking. "Sure. What do you think we should do?"

He put his hand on my shoulder.

"We're going to build a *war room*," he said. "Everywhere you look, I want you to have scripture in front of you. When you brush your teeth, when you're cleaning the dishes, when you walk out that front door. I want you to be continually encouraged by God's promises."

I winced for a moment.

"Well," I said. "I've got these Post-it notes . . ."

And it was then—between the space of him being there and him leaving—that we quickly looked up encouraging scripture, about life, about how God provides, all the best truths that I loved.

The truths that encouraged me.

At first, it felt a little silly. Can I not just read the Bible, Google some scripture when I need it? Why do I need to set up a war room?

But, at this point I was willing to try anything. So, we went to work.

Writing down scripture.

Processing scripture.

Putting it everywhere.

All around my apartment.

On the mirror.

On the fridge.

Everywhere.

The last piece of scripture my dad wrote was from Psalm 91 and it said:

"He is my refuge, and my fortress, and my God, in whom I trust."

This was an incredible exercise, one in which I gained a powerful tool: self-encouragement.

Every morning, when I would look in the mirror to brush my teeth, when I would get dressed, when I would make breakfast, all around me were those encouraging post-it notes.

All I saw was encouragement.

Even more importantly, I started to memorize these passages. They slowly became the soundtrack in my head.

And the more and more I had the words in my mind, the more and more I started to believe them. God's word says that scripture should be written on our heart—*let love and faithfulness never leave you; bind them around your neck, write them on the tablet of your heart (Proverbs 3:3)*.

And it worked.

It actually *worked*.

Slowly, I climbed out of the hole I was in. My feelings of defeat, shame, and failure started to lighten.

The Mind-Altering Power of Your Words

Negative thoughts can pop into our heads, uninvited, a thousand times a day, and it can be challenging to stop them. But how you choose to respond to those thoughts is completely up to you.

There is a really interesting principle that I have come to understand through my own life experiences: we cannot always control the thoughts we think, but we can always control the words we speak, and interestingly, what we speak has the power to shape what we think.

Did you know that our brains possess the power of something called "neuroplasticity?" Neuroplasticity refers to the brain's ability to change, reorganize, and develop new pathways in response to both internal and external inputs, which gives our brain the capacity to grow and evolve based off of life experiences. What's crazy is that the input that influences neuroplasticity can include something as simple as our words and thoughts.

Scientific research has shown that we actually create grooves in our brain with repeated thoughts—it's the brain equivalent of driving your car over the same part of the road every single day and creating ruts in it. And once those ruts are created, it can be really hard to get out of them. So, if you are dwelling consistently in negative thoughts, you create grooves in your brain that make it difficult to think anything besides those negative thoughts. But repeatedly speaking positive words over yourself when negative thoughts come in is one way to create new, more positive ruts. For better or worse, our thoughts and words *physically* change our brain.

The scriptures I wrote down, that I read and reread a hundred times a day, became the positive words that could shape the thoughts that created new pathways in my brain. Every time a negative thought would come in, I could choose to read a scripture, and instead of allowing my thoughts to continue wearing the same anxious rut in my brain, I could create a new one of peace.

This is the power of self-encouragement.

Encouraging others is a vital skill. We need people to spread love in our world, to encourage others, to lift them up. But bigger than that, where it all starts, is our self-encouragement. We are, in many ways, a reflection of our inner world. As you encourage others, you've got to encourage yourself.

This is simple, but it is not easy. We are human and most certainly will have moments of sadness, envy, anger, etc. But if we can be mindful about the lens through which we view the world—the way we speak to ourselves, the ruts we allow our thoughts to form—we will find that even the most difficult situations can become easier to navigate.

Reader Challenge

In Chapter 1, you wrote down the names of 10 people in your life that you are going to encourage using the principles you learn in this book. We are going to spend the next eight chapters encouraging those people, but first I want you to learn how to encourage someone else—yourself.

You cannot speak kindly to the people in your life if you don't learn to speak kindly to yourself—it just won't feel as authentic.

If self-encouragement is not something that comes naturally to you, I have a few simple tips to help you out.

Ed Mylett, a popular motivational speaker, business leader, and TV personality, once taught me an incredibly important lesson: your environmental game drives your mental game. In other words, to set yourself up for success, you first have to set up the right environment. So, in order to be successful with self-encouragement, you need to create an environment of self-encouragement. For me, this looked like decking my apartment out with scripture, creating what I called the "war room." What would it look like for you?

Don't overthink it. Your "war room" can be a few simple truths you speak over yourself daily—positive words that you write down and put in common places you look so you'll start to drive those thoughts in to your head. These can include:

- Sayings of encouragement.
- Ideas that lift you up.
- Concepts that drive you toward positivity, optimism.

The Art of Self-Encouragement

It is important to understand that self-encouragement is not going to happen on its own. You have to be intentional about the ways you act and think and show up in the world. Prior to working on my war room with my dad, I made very little effort to curb the negative thoughts I was having. But if you leave it to chance, your negative voice can continue to unconsciously run the show and wear those deep ruts deeper. In order to self-encourage, you have to create space for it. You need to have an open mind, be willing to slow down, and shape your words into encouraging ones.

Our thoughts naturally trend toward fear, danger, anxiety, worry, frustration. And while these are totally normal parts of the human experience, these things can shape our actual world-view, how we view goals and life experiences. We can't just wish away this reality; we have to take initiative to shape it differently. It takes time, and energy, and effort, and slowing down, to do it.

Create a habit out of this practice of positive speaking and thinking. Choose a time of day or an activity that is connected to specifically reflecting on the words in your head and how you'd like to shift them. For some, the practice of journaling helps carve out a specific window in the day to examine thoughts and reframe them into encouraging ones. Others may find a regular rhythm of praying or talking to themselves works better.

It can feel incredibly unnatural at first. Maybe even a little phoned-in.

But it is worth it. I promise, it really makes a difference.

So, journal (or pray, or say in your own head, or out loud) things that are naturally encouraging:

What accomplishments are you proud of?

What are you grateful for?

What are you excited about?

What did you do right today?

Where did you win?

If you really take the time to answer these types of questions—even when it's hard, even when you're feeling not so encouraged—you will find the positive. Whatever it might be, there's always something to journal, to talk about, to know, to self-encourage yourself with.

Another very practical tip as you reshape the words in your head is to subtract influences that don't encourage positive thinking. The people and influences in the closest proximity to you have the greatest power over you. It may be wise to reduce proximity to toxic people and situations. Stay away from negative news and depressing content. What you allow in your environment will become a part of it and will start to shape your thinking.

Lastly, remember:

It's a practice.

You have to do this consistently and routinely. You have to do it more than just once. I find that when I stay consistent in this practice, I notice a huge difference. When I'm consistently praying, consistently reflecting on those gratitude questions, I see the glass half-full far more often. The more I take time to build my internal "war room," the better I feel, the more productive I am, and the better I am able to encourage and lead others.

I know you'll find the same, too.

Be sure to write down some examples of self-encouragement that you gave yourself in the Observations section for Chapter 2 at the end of the book. How did you feel doing it, and how did you feel after a few days of doing it? Record these experiences!

Chapter 3

The Art of Character Encouragement

Fast-forward about five years. My own personal journey in self-development following the end of my career had grown—as these things so often do—into an opportunity to help others with the same. During my valley season, I basically received a PhD through the school of hard knocks in emotional intelligence, self-awareness, and decision making, amongst other skills, and this learning experience actually gave me a platform to coach and teach. I found myself thriving as a performance coach, helping leaders with personal development in the soft skills, enabling them to become more effective in their leadership journey, better communicators, more aware, and more socially intelligent. I engaged in public speaking, sharing my story, in hopes of helping others learn from my mistakes.

One thing I have learned in my coaching career is the importance of recognizing someone for their character—their innate attributes, moral qualities, principles, and personality traits that make them the unique being that they are. A person's character is essentially their essence—it's what makes them, them! While character is completely unique to each person, their skillset— the collection of capabilities and proficiencies that they can gain through training—is something that anybody can possess, and it inherently feels less special when they are recognized for it. When you praise and encourage a person in their character, you are making them feel like they are wonderful because of *who* they are, rather than *what* they do, and it is this feature that makes the Art of Character Encouragement so impactful!

The Phone Call

Today, as someone who talks for a living, I don't often lack for things to say. Although my friends have been known to give me a hard time for that quality, it has made being a keynote speaker and performance coach a natural fit for me because I don't worry about what I might say in new situations. That was, until I got a call—a call I will never forget—to work with a professional athlete I had admired for years.

For all my life, I've been invested in the sports world. Growing up in small town Iowa, sports were everything to me. Sports were intricately woven into the fabric of my school experience, they were the center of the conversations I had with friends, the dreams we had of what we wanted to do when we grew up, nearly all of it was built around our love of sports.

As a personal development coach, I had had several opportunities to work with sports teams, helping players to grow in their skills to become better leaders and teammates. But there was a pivotal moment in time where I found myself working for the first time with someone who was a renowned athlete in the world of pro sports.

That moment began with a call from my friend Ross.

"Brandon is going to call you. Would that be okay?"

I realized, without a shadow of a doubt, that when he said Brandon, he meant Brandon Scherff, one of the most tenured and successful players in the NFL. A former first round draft pick, and a five-time NFL All Pro offensive lineman. As a devout football fan, I deeply respected Brandon as a player.

Ross thought I could help Brandon with his mental game, improving his mindset and growing his leadership skills. This could be a huge opportunity to combine two of my greatest passions—personal development and sports—and I definitely couldn't miss it.

But when it came time for our first phone call, I was admittedly a little nervous. Coaching someone of Brandon's caliber was a pretty big step in my personal development coaching career. It was hard to feel adequately prepared to coach a pro athlete at an All-Pro level—one of the best in the world at what he does.

Brandon's name popped up on my cell phone. I took a deep breath and answered.

"Hey Jordan. How are you?"

I'm not sure what I was expecting, to be honest, but I guess I didn't expect the conversation to begin like any other. I thought he would be incredibly particular. I thought he was going to want to talk strategy, I thought it would feel intense and intimidating. But it was soon clear that everything I thought we were going to talk about, we wouldn't talk about.

We discussed life, parenting, marriage. It was like talking to an old friend.

At one point, he asked me: "Got any books?"

I was confused. I didn't know what he meant, and I paused for a moment.

"Books? Like that I've written?" I asked stupidly.

"No . . . ," he said. "Books that I should read?"

Right.

An area I am so well-versed in for coaching, in that moment I found myself floundering and thinking *well, jeez, I have no idea what he is in to.*

But as we continued talking, it became entirely clear that Brandon—the Brandon I had admired for so long—was as easy to talk to as my small-town Iowa buddies. He was kind and genuine. Humble and thoughtful.

And before I knew it, we had ended the call and never even spoke a word about football.

The Servant Leader

After that initial meeting with Brandon, I was able to make it to a game and meet him in person. It was a Monday Night Football game pitting Brandon's Washington Commanders against the high-flying Seattle Seahawks. The Commanders found themselves on the winning end of a 17-15 victory, their fifth of the season.

After the game, I had the opportunity to head to the players' parking lot to spend some time with Brandon and his teammates, celebrating their win. Lamborghinis, Ferraris, Mercedes, and Bentleys lined the lot—definitely not the same as the ones I rode home in after *my* football games. The players walking to these cars were dressed to the nines, wearing expensive clothes, jewelry, and watches.

But Brandon was different.

Clad in a standard team-issued sweat suit—"this one's free," he grinned—Brandon handed out drinks and moved about the parking lot checking on everyone, seeing if they needed anything, making sure they felt comfortable and included.

He was so sure of himself. Authentic. Genuine. Perfectly content to help serve others. I sensed that he didn't have to, or want to, change for anybody.

Brandon's humble take on life completely changed my perspective that evening. He didn't seem concerned about football or the fame of it all. He was just being himself and who God made him to be. All of the glitter and gold of his being a professional football player started to fade. I started to see Brandon and his teammates for *who* they were, instead of just for *what* they did.

Thinking back on that game I can't remember many details of the plays I watched, the points scored. Instead, what left a lasting impression was Brandon's character, and in the coming years of working together, it was this beautiful character that I would continually strive to encourage in my coaching with Brandon.

Even Elite Performers Need Encouragement

Brandon and I continued to work together over the following months.

We had developed a friendship, and I knew what he needed most from me from a coaching perspective. Anyone under the sun could talk to him about football. But I was

35

there for the conversations about life. I was there to listen and support him through a physically and emotionally draining high-profile career, and to help him balance that career with being a full-time husband and father. That's where I could make the biggest impact.

One day Brandon called me, and I could tell something was off. His voice was different.

"Hey man, what's up?" I said.

"I'm sideways." Brandon said.

He's not one to pull punches, he just cuts right to the chase. I'd grown to appreciate that about Brandon. If he had something on his mind, he said it immediately.

Brandon proceeded, "normally I stay away completely from reading these sorts of critical pieces during the season, but I accidentally bumped into this thing . . . ," and he went on to tell me about an analyst who had written an article about his performance. Not a positive article. The analyst had critiqued a recent game and highlighted things in Brandon's performance he thought suggested that the lineman was struggling.

Of course, this was just one game and just one analyst's opinion, but for Brandon, that didn't stop the words from stinging.

I knew it wasn't true. Not even close. In fact, he was having another All-Pro season. In my opinion, Brandon had absolutely nothing to worry about.

But it was still hitting a pain point for Brandon, and you could tell the words had shaken him. Anyone reading something negative about themselves would be bothered the way Brandon was, and I knew exactly what he needed.

"Let's jump right to it," I said. "I want to zoom out with you a little bit. Forget about that article. Let's talk about who you really are."

Silence. I could tell he was a little surprised that I wasn't going to dissect the facts in the article.

I went ahead.

"You're a former first round draft pick. You're a team captain, AND you're a five-time All-Pro offensive lineman. Your football career has been legendary. I mean, you are one of the best to ever do what you've done. You're one of the best athletes on the planet."

I was picking up speed.

"More importantly, you are an incredible, loving father," I said. "You are a great husband. You are surrounded by a community who you love and who loves you back. Your family is amazing and engaged. You have one of the biggest hearts of anyone I have ever met, and you have this inspiring ability to remain humble, sincere, and down-to-earth, despite your incredible success. So tell me, are you going to let this reporter—this guy, who's sitting behind a computer in New York City, an analyst, who doesn't know you, who's never met you, who has *opinions* for a living—are you going to let him dictate who you believe yourself to be?"

I felt intense, demonstrative.

"This freakin' guy—," I said. "This freakin' analyst who doesn't know you?"

There was a silence for a moment. And then a chuckle on the other end of the line.

"Well," Brandon said. "You know . . . *when you put it like that . . .*"

We laughed. And in that moment, I was reminded that what Brandon needed was what we all need as human beings. We need to be reminded of who we really are, and who we have the potential to be.

We need to be encouraged.

Sometimes we need an audible voice to remind us of what we already know. It is in moments like these I am reminded that encouragement doesn't have to be groundbreaking. Sometimes you can simply remind people of what they already know to be true. It's incredibly powerful, and it's incredibly simple.

As easy as it can be to get caught up in believing that some people have "graduated" from needing encouragement, that somehow their influence or their role excludes them from this basic need, it is fundamentally not true. We are all just people. And people need encouragement.

The Who Over the Do—Character Encouragement

True encouragement, like the encouragement I offered Brandon in his moment of insecurity, prioritizes recognition of the *who*, over the *do*. In other words, you praise someone because of their character—the characteristics and behaviors that make them unique—instead of praising them for their skills.

It is far easier to praise performance, status, achievement— what someone *does*—over *who* they really are. Trust me, I have struggled with this myself many times, and I still have to work at it even today. As we find ourselves leading people—whether at work, on the field, or at home—we can easily fall into the trap of providing recognition only surrounding the metrics of someone's performance. It is all too easy to provide encouragement based off of what they contribute to the bottom line.

Because this type of surface-level encouragement is so easy, almost reflexive, I find that companies' cultures are often plagued with this issue. It's easy to look at the team member who exceeded their sales goal for the month and give them a pat on the back. In fact, they've probably come to expect that kind of praise.

And of course, this type of encouragement is not all bad. For businesses, teams, and families it certainly matters that people follow through on expectations and the things they are "required" to do. It would be crazy of me as a performance coach to sit here and tell you that results *don't* matter.

But a person's character, the essence of who they are, their unique traits, qualities, and what they care about, matters far more than all of their skills. When it comes to culture, to encouragement, even to performance, tapping into *who* someone is, is what activates their potential.

If we want to build better teams, improve company culture, shepherd our families, sell more products, win more games, etc., we have to invest time in understanding the unique characteristics that make people who they are, what drives them, what gives them meaning. Then, we find ways to praise that by engaging in the Art of Character Encouragement.

Every once in a while, I will hear a leader mention that it becomes difficult to offer praise to a lackluster team member. In these situations, we must remember that every person brings an element of value connected to their character. Maybe they aren't the most productive or enjoyable team members, but it might be that they add drive, precision-level focus, energy, curiosity, creativity, etc. If you are focused on character, you will find it!

Perhaps this truth is obvious. After all, most of us know that we like to be recognized for who we are, so why wouldn't our team? But if it makes so much sense in theory, why then does it happen so little in practice? Usually, it is because leaders are not taking the time to really learn about who their employees, players, or teammates are. Instead, they are driven by society's metric-based culture. Frankly, it's easier to pay attention to the scores. It's easier to point to the percentages, the sales numbers, the quantitative data—and equate that with who people really are.

But when we connect with a person's character, when we take the time to truly understand them, it changes the way people perform. It connects to their inner need to be known. It makes them feel supported and valued. When encouragement focuses on numbers, when it focuses only on what someone provides quantitatively, it makes them feel interchangeable. They don't necessarily feel seen or understood. They may not feel inspired or appreciated. It's possible, they will leave that workplace in search of one that appreciates them more.

Think back to your workplace or team experiences. Do you remember some of the leaders and mentors who had the greatest impact on you? Who inspired you the most? Was it the leaders that focused on what you could do for them, or the ones that actually cared about who you were? That knew you? That encouraged and loved you?

This is one of my favorite topics to tackle when I'm speaking to various companies on the topic of encouragement. To help drive the message home, I'll often pick someone out in the crowd, someone I have at least some semblance of a relationship with—whether it's the president of the company, the meeting organizer, or the person who served as my point of contact— and specifically recognize them for their unique character.

If I am lucky, there is someone in the audience that I know well personally. This happened for me recently as I was presenting to West Bank—a first class organization in southeast Iowa. They are widely considered one of the top businesses in the area and are well known for community impact and commitment to serving their customers. The local Market President Jim Conard was there and is a close friend of mine. Jim is extremely accomplished; he has grown the bank's presence significantly and is one of the most well-respected leaders in our part of the state. He seems to be on every board and behind every meaningful initiative in our region.

I was a few minutes into my presentation to a room packed full of West Bank leaders, employees, and board members—a very smart, distinguished, and established audience that could easily dismiss my humble and simple message of "who over do." It was the perfect opportunity, and I leaned right into it.

"Jim Conard is with us today! Jim continues to be one of the most accomplished leaders in the Corridor. He was recently voted one of the most influential leaders by the Corridor Business Journal, and the bank is flourishing under his leadership!" I went on to describe some of Jim's accomplishments and the impressive bank results he is responsible for driving. The room smiled. Some small claps ensued. Jim looked at me from the audience with a sheepish grin, a little embarrassed.

I continued right on.

"Hey, I'd like to point out something else about Jim . . . Jim is one of the kindest people I have ever met. He's generous, loyal, and considerate—in fact, he might be one of the most thoughtful people walking this planet. I love his gift of discernment, he's one of the best friends to take advice from—it's always genuine and delivered with care. I have watched him show great kindness to people who didn't deserve it."

The mood in the room started to shift. I watched many heads nodding—others wanting to reaffirm these validating words about Jim. And I wasn't finished yet.

"Jim has a grace about him—he is always choosing to see the best in others and more importantly, helps others see the best in themselves. He's the kind of person everyone wants to be around. He's a people magnet, a connector, a mentor, and a friend to many. You see, Jim is so much more than an accomplished business leader. He's a great husband to Jennifer, and a loving father to his daughter, Meadow."

I walked a bit closer to Jim, my tone firm. I wanted Jim to know that I meant every word I said. Jim is not one for emotion, but I watched his eyes change a bit.

"I love you Jim, and I love that you are achieving results at West Bank, but let's be clear—it is *who* you are that is allowing you to *do* what you do. God made you special, keep being you."

The crowd roared with applause. I gave Jim a smile and put my hand over my heart to demonstrate exactly where my words were coming from.

I will never know exactly how Jim felt in that moment, but I know how I felt. It felt good to share that with Jim, to acknowledge his God-given character and the ways in which he had stewarded his unique gifts. There is a relational and emotional currency and that is different when we are encouraging in the realm of the *who*. It is a far more meaningful way to say "I see you. I notice. You matter." I get to watch rooms change. The applause is different. The emotion is different. Because it *is* different when you praise the *who*.

When you encourage people in their character, you are offering so much more than a simple act of praise. You are not just encouraging them. You are reaffirming the person God made them to be. You are shining a spotlight on their gifts. You are depositing motivation and determination. You can change how they see themselves and how much impact they think they can have on the world.

Everyone has gifts and abilities and talents in a variety of ways. Everyone has something beautiful about their character.

Choose to see the best in people.

Choose to see the "Who" over the "Do."

Choose to shine a light on the best of people, every day.

The world is full of darkness—but you have the spotlight.

Reader Challenge

In Chapter 1, you wrote down the names of 10 people in your life that you are going to encourage using the principles you learn in this book, and this is your opportunity to do exactly that!

For each of the 10 people you chose—your "encouragees"—I want you to encourage them about something having to do with their character and who they are, rather than what they do. This will take some thought, because it is so much easier to praise someone's actions than their intrinsic characteristics. But once you get the hang of it, it will become easier and more natural for you.

Let's move through some examples to help you get a feel for what this type of encouragement might look like:

If your spouse wakes up early with the kids so that you can sleep in, rather than saying "I appreciate you getting up with the kids this morning," try something like "NAME—I truly appreciate your selfless heart. You so often put the kids' needs and mine above your own. You are truly one of the most generous and loving parents I know."

Doesn't that feel so much deeper? There was nothing wrong with the first response, but the second one is clearly more impactful!

Let's try another example. Maybe you have a college intern at your work who hasn't quite figured out the ropes but brings incredible joy and morale to the team. Rather than encouraging them by saying "don't worry, you'll learn X skill in no time," you can say, "NAME, your humor and your energy are contagious. Anyone can learn a skill, but few people have a personality like yours that just naturally brightens the room! Since you have joined our company, your coworkers' morale has drastically increased—you have been such a valuable addition to our team!"

Or perhaps with the waitperson who knows you as a "regular" at your favorite lunch spot: "NAME—I just want to thank you for always making my dining experience such a positive one. You are detail oriented, and you work hard to make sure every last thing is just right. I appreciate your servant's heart. You are truly one of the most committed people I know, and I have really loved having the opportunity to watch you bloom where you are planted. You are making a difference here!"

Got the idea?

This may not feel natural for you at first, and I would encourage you to add your own style. Your most authentic when your most effective!

In the Observations section for Chapter 3, write down the encouraging words you used to praise the 10 people you committed to encourage. Write each person's name, and what you said to them (paraphrasing is okay). How did they respond? How did you feel doing it? What did you notice as you engaged in this exercise with that person? Make sure to write it all down!

Chapter 4

The Art of Consistent Encouragement

In the weeks that followed my termination, I found myself
screening a lot of calls and texts. My whole life, I had been
a people person—I loved connecting with friends and family,
and it was rare to miss a call or not call back. But finding myself
explaining and re-explaining my situation to dozens of people countless times a day was emotionally exhausting and not
sustainable.

Unfortunately for me, my firing was very public and naturally people wanted to know about it. Friends, family members,
colleagues, and clients; the constant communication was difficult to get away from. I never knew whether a phone call would
turn sour, or force me to rehash the story *yet again*. The easiest
solution was to simply ignore them all.

But my friend, Rob Victor, was persistent. He called me day,
after day, after day. For a while, I simply ignored his calls like I
did everyone else's. But where others had been deterred by my
silence, Rob seemed to be fueled by it.

Finally I answered, with the intent of (nicely) telling Rob to
please leave me alone.

I jumped in before he could say anything. "Rob—I love you.
But I can't talk," I said. "My world is falling apart. I see that
you've called me a few times, but I just need some time."

To be honest, I was hoping for him to just hang up.

But instead, in a light-hearted, caring tone, he just said "Dude . . . it's all good. I'm just calling to tell you that I love you, and I'm going to call you every single day to check on you, and remind you that I am thinking of you. When you're ready to talk, we can talk."

And he meant it.

Rob continued to call me, every single day, just as he said he would. Often, I didn't answer, but occasionally I did. Eventually, I began to let down my guard with him.

During one of our conversations Rob said something I have never forgotten:

"You're getting a gift at 27 years old that most people won't get until they're older—it's the gift of finding out who your real friends are. Who loves you because of who you are, and who loves you because of your status, your position, and your work."

The friends that matter aren't the ones that just like you because you did something "cool." They're not the people that like how much money you make. They're not the people that care about your position, or your title, or what you do for a living. Instead, they value you as a person. They are there for you in your worst moments, even when your mistakes and shortcomings have been put on public display. You can do this by doing what Rob did for me—day after day, keep encouraging. Prove it over time. Stay consistent.

The Superpower of Consistency

I would like to ask you once more to think about your own valley experience.

Now, recall the initial response from others in your life. Likely, there was a bit of a rally around you. A recognition that something hard had happened and that you might need help. It can actually be a beautiful and inspiring time: people are there for you, and they're supportive. They call you; they check in on you; they send you condolences.

But then time passes. People start checking in less and less until you hear almost nothing.

You start to feel like you're all by yourself.

This is because we as people tend to forget how powerful consistency can be.

Now translate this to your workplace. Think about the last time you were encouraged or offered encouragement to someone else at work. Most of us can remember someone offering a kind word, an inspirational message, something that lifted us up. But unfortunately, that type of encouragement is often few and far between. It is rarely consistent.

Like everything else we do in life—being consistent is a superpower. What you do every day matters more than what you do every once in a while.

The Chief Reminding Officer

Andy Stanley, founder and senior pastor of North Point Ministries, has said a quote that I absolutely love:

"The cost of under-communicating will be far more significant than the cost of over-communicating."

Meaning: you can over-communicate, repeat yourself a little too much, and risk that people find you a little annoying.

Or—

You can under-communicate, and fail entirely to get your message across.

Which is worse? Personally, I would rather be a little bit annoying than apathetic.

Truthfully, through my many years of coaching leaders in the boardroom and on the field, I have found that it is quite challenging to over-communicate. In fact, the average person needs to hear something seven to eight times before it sticks. So one of our greatest tools as leaders is to be the reminder. My friend Pat Lencioni is a renowned expert in the field of business and particularly team management. Something he regularly coaches his clients on is that a leader's primary role should be as the CRO—Chief Reminding Officer. Simply, put, leaders are repeaters.

Most people don't want to repeat themselves. Most people want something new, or fresh, or interesting to say. But the reality is that encouragement doesn't have to be flashy or new, it just has to be consistent. You have to make sure there is no question whether or not you care. Whether you're coaching a professional basketball team, a team at work, or your little ones at home, stay on repeat.

Reader Challenge

In Chapter 1, you wrote down the names of 10 people in your life that you wanted to encourage using the principles you learn in this book, and in Chapter 3 you had your first opportunity to begin encouraging them in a deeper, more meaningful way. Now, with Chapter 4, you get to build on the practice of encouraging others by showing up for your 10 people when they need it the most.

The most important way to show that you are authentic about the encouragement you are offering others is to be consistent about offering it. So, as uncomfortable as it might feel, I want you to work on finding ways to repeat the encouragement you offered to your 10 people in Chapter 3. You can change up the wording, but keep the message the same.

Your spouse doesn't need to hear that they are selfless and generous just once, and never hear it from you again for the next 10 years. They should hear it every day! That intern at work? They'll probably have made some new mistake this week, and will need to be reminded of the value they offer again. The waitperson at your favorite lunch spot? Maybe they're feeling uncertain of their future—remind them that they are making a difference by blooming where they are planted today!

Write down your experience in practicing the art of consistency in the Observations section at the back of the book! How did people respond to this type of consistent encouragement? How did you feel doing it? Have you started to become more comfortable with this practice yet? Are the words coming more naturally to you? Record it all!

You'll practice this skill of consistent encouragement throughout the rest of the book, and hopefully the rest of your life, so I suggest you lean into any discomfort you experience with repeating yourself and learn to embrace it. It will only bring positive change to your communication!

Chapter 5

The Art of Caring Encouragement

In this chapter, we will dive into examples in my own life of the Art of Caring Encouragement, and provide simple but effective ways to demonstrate it in the lives of those around you. First though, it is important to understand the foundation of the art of care—a determination to make others feel valued, appreciated, seen, and loved, without requiring anything in return from them.

We have an amazing example of the power of this profound, selfless care, in the scriptures written by our loving God, which offer us the ultimate encouragement as believers. We are able to care on such a deep level for others because our eternal Father cares for us. Psalm 37:23 puts this loving care on display: "The Lord directs the steps of the godly. He delights in every detail of their lives."

Perhaps one of the most convincing passages that details God's depth of caring for us is Luke 12:6–7: "Are not five sparrows sold for two pennies? And not one of them is forgotten before God. Why, even the hairs of your head are all numbered. Fear not; you are of more value than many sparrows." So, if God remembers and thinks about the common, valueless birds that people sell for a pittance, how much more does He care for

His children? And Matthew 6:25–33 provides us with the same message. Here, Jesus counsels against worry about our circumstances, illuminating the amazing truth that God provides for birds and flowers, things that pass quickly and are considered insignificant and fleeting to us as humans. How much more must He care for His people?

This ultimate example of loving care should inspire us as leaders, who in their faith hope to imitate God—the ultimate Leader. If I do nothing else in life, I will know I have succeeded if I've loved others well. If I've been kind and caring, if I've listened, shared my faith, and tried to love like God loves, then I will have had a life worth living.

To me, true caring is the highest form of encouragement and is the ultimate hallmark of a great leader—a leader that others want to follow. When people know that you care about them, there's nothing more powerful than that.

The Caring Encourager

Tim Bohannon was—in common parlance—"the man." Known as a very wise and discerning leader, steadfast, dynamic, humble, and consistent, Tim is a people magnet. People naturally want to follow him. At the time, he had roughly 30 years of leadership experience in the financial services industry, and he was a managing partner of the company I had just been fired from—covering the Minneapolis, Minnesota branch.

And he was calling me.

It wasn't the most convenient timing. I was in the middle of trying to get a hold of the bank, as I had some bills I wasn't going to be able to pay, but something told me that Tim's phone call was one I would want to take the time to answer.

"Jordan!" he said. As usual, Tim's enthusiasm was infectious. Just hearing his voice and energy as he said my name made me smile. It was exactly what I needed.

We took a few minutes to catch up before Tim asked a question that took me by complete surprise: "Would you ever consider coming to work for us here in Minneapolis?"

For context, in my small little world of the financial services sector, this was like Phil Jackson of the '97 Bulls asking if I'd come play next to Michael Jordan. Tim was at the top of his game in the financial services industry, one of the most successful leaders in the industry, a living legend, and the opportunity to work alongside him was an incredible opportunity for a second chance. I would be crazy not to say yes.

In a matter of days, I was in Minneapolis to see if the opportunity was a good fit. Tim took me around the city, showing me his favorite spots. In a season of feeling a bit like damaged goods, Tim was rolling out the metaphorical red carpet for me. Not because I was some big-time recruit, but simply because he was being kind and compassionate to a young man he knew was hurting. Suddenly, I had a seat at the table again.

I felt the weight lift.

As we sat down to dinner together one evening, I opened up to Tim about how I had been struggling since my (very public) firing.

"Man," Tim said, "let's just focus on helping you move forward." Spoken like a true coach.

That evening Tim brought optimism, hope, and enthusiasm back into my life. He had the remarkable ability to cast a vision for me when I couldn't see it myself. Taking a job with Tim was a no-brainer, and over the next two years that I worked with him, he continued to be every bit as kind and positive as that first interaction.

Tim was an unusual boss. He regularly checked in with me during my employment with him, but he very seldom wanted to know about my business results, which was interesting, considering that we were in the business of making results happen.

I can so distinctly remember the types of questions he *did* ask:

How was I doing? In my personal life, relationally, spiritually?

Do I feel like I'm learning anything?

Do I feel valued? Appreciated?

What could be done better?

It was such a sweet season of rebuilding for me. As Craig Groeschel, pastor of Life Church and well-known author, says "sometimes God has to do something *in* you, before He does something *with* you." I experienced this firsthand during this time. I learned to accept feedback, and started actively asking for it. I prayed more often. I slowed down. I started to trust God's plan for my life, and began to see the bigger picture of how He was working in my circumstances to reshape my heart, teaching me the power of gratitude and appreciation. What really mattered in life became more and more clear to me.

My actions began to more closely align with my core values. I started putting time and energy into what really mattered.

So much of that transformation was made possible by Tim and his cast of an all-star team—BJ Hellyer, Lauren McCormick, Joel Molitor, and Jordan Haulke, among others. The more Tim asked me those big picture life questions, the more I realized the everyday results were not what mattered most. He continuously supported and cast a bigger vision for me—one that went beyond what I could offer his company—to help me see what I could offer this *world*. I began to believe in a brighter future for myself.

Tim's caring encouragement in this period of my life helped me get back onto the path God had already laid out for me. It remains to this day one of the most significant examples I personally have of the life-changing power of encouragement.

But Tim's natural giftedness as an encouraging leader would soon become even more apparent.

Like all seasons in life, eventually the winds changed, and after a couple of years of working for Tim, I found myself needing to move back to Iowa in order to pursue a relationship with the woman who would eventually become my wife, Ashley.

I needed to talk to Tim about it, and it was a conversation I deeply dreaded.

The 20-minute drive to the office that morning felt like an eternity. As is human nature, I was playing the conversation over and over in my head, trying to prepare myself for Tim to be severely disappointed in me. Despite the selfless concern, care, and encouragement that Tim had offered me over my years with him, I was sure that this time, I was asking too much, and he would be upset. I could barely stand the thought of hurting someone who had been so kind and generous with me. Financially, I had not earned enough yet for the company to justify the expense Tim had taken on by hiring me and paying for my relocation, and I felt deeply guilty about it. I was sure that this decision would sour our relationship.

"J-mo!" Tim said, enthusiastic as ever as I walked into his office. "Hey bud!"

My heart sank. This was going to be even harder than I thought. Tim sat patiently with me, waiting for me to speak.

"Tim," I said. "I don't know how to tell you this."

My chest felt tight.

"You have been so radically generous with me, and I owe so much to you," I started, "but I am falling more in love with Ashley, and I don't know what to do . . . she's—she's in Iowa, and—"

I couldn't even say what I'd wanted to say.

Without missing a beat, Tim jumped in.

"Well then, you should move back to Iowa," he said, smiling kindly.

I felt a little stunned. It wasn't that easy.

Yeah, but—," I said. "You've given me so much, your time, energy, resources, staff, office space, everything . . . ."

I didn't want to disappoint him. I was paralyzed by the enormity of the decision facing me.

"I don't know," I said. "If I can do that to you."

Tim smiled again.

"Sure you can, Jordan" he said. "You can do anything you want to do."

And just like that, Tim once again graciously exhibited his ever-reliable, selfless, caring encouragement, this time setting me free to move back to Iowa, marry my wife, and start the family I had longed for. Tim was demonstrating the art of care.

What an incredible example he was setting for me. An example that, in time, would shape my own heart as a leader.

Show It, Don't Tell It

During the two years I worked with Tim, he frequently repeated the phrase: "Show me, don't tell me."

The truth is that what you do will always be more powerful than what you say. Talk is cheap. Action is real.

In working with Tim, I learned in more than one way that people can hear your words, but they *feel* your actions. This single principle taught me so much of what I needed to know in order to conduct myself, my life, and my business with integrity and authenticity.

Tim was an example of what it means to walk your talk. He didn't just *say* that he cared about me. He didn't just offer some half-hearted inspirational words to make me feel good and motivate me so that I would be more productive. He actually cared. He showed it, every day, in the best ways possible. Even when it made no sense for him from a business perspective, he cared enough to support what was best for me as a person, and not as an employee.

It was one of the most profound moments of my life, because it cemented a fact I already knew—that I was more to Tim than just an employee. I was family. A forever friend.

When you're a leader—whether in a company, a family, or a team—you can certainly get by with mostly relying on your words to convey what you feel. But, in reality, if you want to be a leader that people truly want to follow, then your actions have to match your words, and action requires effort in a way that words rarely do.

If someone comes to you with their difficult situation, do you simply respond, "I'll be praying for you" or "I'll be thinking of you"? Or are you taking concrete steps to engage in helping that person?

When we're busy and stressed it can be quite challenging to put a pause in the middle of our day to do something nice for someone. In our world it is far easier to say than it is to do. I will say it again: action takes effort. It often requires you to give up your time and your energy to be there for someone in a real way, and yet, that's what sets it apart and makes it so vital.

Tim Bohannon demonstrated this level of care by calling me up, checking on me, taking me around the city and out to dinner. He demonstrated it by taking a chance on me and offering me a chance to rebuild my life and my reputation with him. It was a tremendous energetic and financial investment that Tim took on to hire me, and one of the most important things it accomplished in my life was showing me an example of the incredible impact of caring encouragement.

These actions don't always have to be big, grand gestures.

Sometimes the art of care is something as simple as taking the time to write an encouraging note to someone rather than just "liking" their social media post. Or perhaps it takes the shape of a quick phone call just to check in on how someone is doing. Maybe you offer to help the person in some way, run an errand for them, or make them a meal, or do something that makes their life easier.

Several years ago, I had the fortune of watching someone who was a master of encouragement put incredibly thoughtful effort into a simple, but impactful, gesture of caring encouragement for my wife, Ashley.

Ashley and I operate our business together. My running joke (which is actually not really a joke) is that I run my mouth, and she runs the business. Ashley is a tireless worker, a get-stuff-done kind of woman. While I talk and interact on the front end, Ashley is the glue that's keeping it all together. Not everyone notices that dynamic, but it is an important part of our business structure. I do my best to recognize and encourage Ashley whenever I have the opportunity, but because of the behind-the-scenes nature of her job, it's not often that she gets the recognition she truly deserves.

In the beginning stages of starting Montgomery Companies, I was asked by a managing partner at Northwestern Mutual Indiana, Dave Kiecker, to come out to visit his office for an overnight retreat. We were going to discuss working together and potentially doing some consulting work with his firm. I had known and respected Dave for a long time, so I was thrilled at the opportunity to spend this time with him and his leadership team. Throughout the day, true to his nature, Dave demonstrated an extraordinary level of care for me, but it was what happened later that really blew me away.

It was late afternoon the next day after the retreat, and I was heading home when I got a call from Ashley.

The Art of Caring Encouragement

"You're never going to believe it . . . ," she started. "There's this gorgeous bouquet of flowers on the kitchen table . . ."

"Let me guess," I said. "They're from Dave."

Inside the flowers was a little note:

"Ashley—thank you for letting us steal Jordan the last twenty-four hours. God bless."

It was one of the most thoughtful gestures I have ever had the privilege to witness. Dave truly went out of his way to make Ashley feel cared for. This level of thoughtful care is rare these days, and it's something neither of us will ever forget.

A Leader with a Heart

So, what does caring have to do with encouragement? With being a leader?

As Craig Groeschel puts it:

"People would rather follow a leader with a heart than a leader with a title."

When people know that you really care about who they are, they want to do the best they possibly can for you. They want to succeed, and make you proud. They want to work with you, and will listen to you. Caring for others is where the power to offer them true encouragement comes from.

We live in a world where we're quick to give advice. When someone comes to us for help, we offer them a strategy, an idea, or a new way forward. But what people really need is not a quick fix; and we are not in charge of fixing them anyway. The best thing we can actually do for them? Love them, encourage them, care for them. Be there for them. Treat them well. Help them feel seen and heard.

This is what Tim did for me that night at dinner when I opened up about my problems. He listened, quietly, patiently. He didn't interject with his own thoughts or advice; he gave me space to speak. And then at the end of it, he simply said, "let's just focus on helping you move forward." It was exactly what I needed, and Tim was a wise man to see that at the time.

Bob Goff is a well-loved public speaker and author of *The New York Times* best-selling books *Love Does* and *Everybody, Always*. One of my favorite ideas that he has shared is that most people need to be loved more than they need advice.

A great way to *show* others that you are there for them is to ask them questions that can help you understand how to best be there for them:

How can I support you?

What do you need from me?

What can I help you with?

This is so much more powerful that doling out advice.

Don't get me wrong, there is a time and place for strategy and tactical discussions, but we are all flooded with people who are willing to provide that kind of "help." What is far more impactful, is true caring.

I often think back to my interaction with Tim when I was leaving for Iowa. Tim didn't stand to gain a single thing business-wise from being kind to me in that moment. In fact, from a business perspective he stood to lose the money he had invested in me. But he cared for me so much more than any money gained or lost, and in doing so, he showed me that he cared about Jordan the person rather than Jordan the employee.

True caring means showing up because you care about the person as a person. No strings attached.

As Goethe said: "You can easily judge the character of a man by how he treats those who can do nothing for him."

Reader Challenge

For your 10 "encouragees," in this reader challenge we are going to practice the Art of Caring Encouragement, and one of the most impactful ways to do that is to offer yourself up to them in a gesture of selfless support.

As we discussed in this chapter, these actions don't always have to be big, grand gestures. Sometimes it is something as simple as taking the time to write an encouraging note to someone rather than just "liking" their social media post. Or perhaps it takes the shape of a quick phone call just to check in on how someone is doing. Maybe you offer to help the person in some way, run an errand for them, or make them a meal, or do something that makes their life easier.

There are no hard and fast rules. Caring is often simply spelled T-I-M-E.

I understand that between the space of this chapter and the next, you might not have time to make 10 different people meals or write 10 different hand-written notes. Remember that we are playing the long game here, and that lends itself more to a "slow and steady wins the race" sort of approach rather than a series of short, intense sprints. Maybe leave your favorite waitperson an extra-large tip this week, or ask the check-out person at the grocery store how things are going for them in their personal life, whether at school or work or in their family (as long as this won't be perceived as creepy—let's use discernment here).

Ask your encouragee what they are passionate about in life, and listen attentively to them when they tell you about it (bonus—you'll use this information for your reader challenge in the Art of Illuminating Encouragement). The next time you talk to that person, follow up on this conversation and ask how things are progressing—nothing demonstrates care like remembering what is important to others and showing a vested interest in the outcomes of their efforts.

Write down what acts of caring you demonstrated for your 10 encouragees in the space provided for Chapter 5 observations at the back of the book. What stood out the most to you in this exercise? Did you find it harder, or easier, than you expected to have a deeper-level conversation with these individuals? What new and surprising things did you learn about your encouragees' lives? How did they respond to you showing this deeper level of care for them? Document it all!

Chapter 6

The Art of Energetic Encouragement

I loved high school. As an adult, I hear so many people describe their high school experience as awkward or drama filled. For me, that wasn't the case. I loved being around so many different people with different perspectives, different walks of life. Even in small town Iowa, walking down the high school hallways, I noticed people who looked different, sounded different, *were* different.

I often found those hallways a bit of a reprieve, in fact. At the time, I was walking through the hardest thing I had experienced in my short time on earth—my mom and dad were getting a divorce. Enduring the fallout and complications from our family unit looking different was a lot for a teenager to manage, so school was something I looked forward to each day. I got to see my best friends daily, play sports with them, goof around with them. I was constantly around people I knew and loved, and it was a great distraction from the difficulties I was facing in my personal life.

Football was another positive distraction for me at the time. My assistant coach, Jay Bickford, was a rock in my life. He was in his early thirties, a former Division One offensive lineman at the University of Iowa. He was one of the biggest, strongest, most muscular men I've ever seen, and yet he was also incredibly kind. Before games, during practice, after practice, in the hallways—Coach Bickford just had a positive vibe about him. You always felt good when you were with him. His caring, encouraging nature was on display.

There was one specifically memorable moment before a game where Coach Bickford showed me the incredible power of energetic encouragement. I was with the other captains of the team, stretching and getting warmed up for the game, dressed and ready to go. I felt the usual nervous and excited energy that filled the air before a game.

Out of nowhere, Coach Bickford came walking up to me and grabbed my face mask, bringing his eyes to mine, before yelling directly into my face:

"JORDAN—YOU'RE THE BEST PLAYER ON THIS FIELD! ENJOY THE MOMENT!"

And then he left.

And I was glowing.

Now, was I actually the best high school football player on the team?

Probably not.

But it made me feel like king of the world when he said that to me, and I think Coach Bickford knew it. I think that Coach Bickford knew that I was hurting and confused by what was happening in my life, and that I needed someone to build me up. It didn't matter that in reality I was a no-name high school student that no one in the world actually knew about. He made me believe I was truly the best.

The Art of Encouragement

This level of encouragement was very necessary for me during an otherwise incredibly difficult season of life, where I was dealing with some situations I had no idea how to navigate. I felt insecure in my personal life, in my broken family, but the moment I stepped onto that football field I was transformed into someone else by Coach Bickford's contagious energy. Someone who knew exactly how to handle whatever came their way. It was—quite literally—game-changing, both for my life on the field, and my life at home.

For the next nine Fridays in a row, before every game, Coach would grab my face mask, and every time—

"JORDAN—YOU'RE THE BEST PLAYER ON THIS FIELD!"

I was a scrawny high school kid, but I felt like Walter Payton. Coach Bickford was empowering me with his energy.

People hear your words. But they *feel* your attitude and your energy. Coach Bickford's words might not have been a realistic representation of my actual performance on the field, but the truth is, it didn't matter. I *loved* Coach Jay. I *still* love him. He was one of the most impactful people in my young life, and that underscores an important point:

It's not *what* you say that makes the difference.

It's *how* you make people feel.

One of my favorite aphorisms that I am constantly reminding my clients of is that amateurs focus on what they're going to say, but professionals focus on how they're going to say it.

The Art of Energetic Encouragement

We frequently spend too much time and effort on the exact words we want to communicate, rather than focusing on how we should communicate it. I am frequently guilty of this myself. But often we are missing it entirely. More than 90% of our communication is non-verbal—posture, hand gestures, facial expression, etc. It's our energy. And in my experience, our energy is more important than anything that comes out of our mouth.

It was this level of infectious energy that Coach Bickford displayed every single game. It wasn't just the words he spoke to me. It was his attitude, his posture, his mannerisms. He had thoroughly convinced me with his short pre-game message throughout the season that I was the best player on the field, a tremendous testament to the encouragement that we can deposit in others not just with *what* we say, but *how* we say it.

As Maya Angelou said: "People won't always remember what you said—but they'll always remember the way you made them feel."

For nine fall Friday nights in small town Iowa, Coach Bickford had gotten a slow-footed 160-pound running-back to believe he was an All-American. His presence, his posture, his tonality, his smile, and everything about his body language communicated the message:

I believe in you.

I support you.

He transferred energy.

And this transfer of encouraging energy is important—for companies, cultures, teams—because what drives belief and what sticks with people, is how you make them feel.

University of Kentucky basketball coach, John Calipari, famously captured the importance of unspoken communication when he shared with a group of coaches the wisdom that "Your body language never whispers—it screams."

American culture overvalues specifics, the know-how, and undervalues posture, the be-how, but some of the most encouraging conversations I've had didn't have many words to them. They were all about actions. In difficult situations, encouragement may look like sitting quietly and listening, holding the person's hand, giving them a hug. In celebratory moments, we clap, we cheer, we high-five, we embrace. Whether we're encouraging someone through a celebratory moment—life's biggest wins—or a tragedy—life's deepest valleys—the most encouraging thing you can do is be present, and be *present*. In other words, be fully there for the person and undistracted from them. I shared the example of Coach Bickford, who was a big, loud, in-your-face guy, because that was an incredibly impactful example of the Art of Energetic Encouragement in my life, but it's important to understand that good energy is not always synonymous with big energy, and it definitely doesn't have to mean loud energy. Good energy means different things for different people. We're all unique, and we're all a little different. That means we all have different energy styles, and you'll encourage best with your own unique energy.

You are most effective when you're most authentic.

The Art of Energetic Encouragement

John Maxwell is an American author, speaker, and pastor. He's considered one of the top authorities on the topic of leadership, and I've had the incredible opportunity to learn from him in a mentoring relationship. When I first got into public speaking, he told me something I won't ever forget: "If you're not funny, don't open your speech with a joke." Maybe that seems obvious, but that advice was so refreshing for me personally, as I had been told by other mentors to get the crowd engaged or laughing by sharing something humorous to open my presentation. The problem is, that's not me, and it comes across as inauthentic when I try. "Instead," John said. "Just be yourself. That's the best way to be."

All too often I think people are not using their energy positively because they've been coached to try to be someone else. To match someone else's style or energy. And it's such a big mistake. You just have to be who you are.

Reader Challenge

In this reader challenge, we are taking the Art of Encouragement to the next level with our energy to make your encouragees feel like the proverbial "BEST PLAYER ON THE FIELD!"

This week, I would challenge you to find ways to show up for your encouragees with authentic energy. You're going to go above and beyond in your encouragement for them, which may feel like a bit of a stretch for you at first, but I promise that with practice, you will get more comfortable doing it. For this challenge, it is important to encourage them in person, so that you can look them in the eye and really engage them with your energy. Slow down, and be intentional. If in person is absolutely not possible, then over the phone will suffice.

I want you to catch the person by surprise with your energy. Tell them that they are amazing at what they do. Make them believe it, just like Coach Bickford did for me! I don't care if they are a bus driver or an All-Pro athlete—they should feel like the king of the world after you are done with them. And in reality, even if they aren't the best at what they do, making them feel good about their abilities can be incredibly trans-formative, giving them the confidence they need to become better at it. This can be simple—"Tracey, you are THE world's BEST accountant—no one can problem-solve like you!"—but remember that simple is no less profound.

Use the Chapter 6 space at the back of the book to record your observations from this exercise. Was it harder, or easier, than you imagined to bring this level of energy to your inter-actions? How did the encouragee respond to this over-the-top encouragement? Did you get eyerolls, or did they seem pleased? There are no right or wrong reactions, even if they act embarrassed or like they don't care. Secretly, everybody likes to be encouraged in this way as long as it comes across as genuine!

Chapter 7

The Art of Illuminating Encouragement

"Who wants to try out for student council? Raise your hand if you want to try out!"

Mrs. Allen, my sixth-grade teacher, posed her question to the class.

She was explaining the whole process. You give a speech, you take a stand on a topic, and then you vote. Simple enough. She recommended we all try it—she said that it would be a great step toward developing yourself, being a leader.

Being a leader sounded awesome to me. How often are we given the chance to wield any sort of power as a twelve-year-old? The more Mrs. Allen talked—positive, bubbly enthusiasm just pouring out of her—the more I started to get excited. Her energy was infectious. It didn't matter that up until about 30 seconds ago, I didn't even know student council existed. I was in.

There was only one problem.

My friends.

I had a few friends who were right behind me, sitting in their desks. Typical sixth-grade boys, just like me. I turned around and glanced at them to see if they were thinking what I was thinking. They definitely weren't. There was only about a foot between us, but I could have read their body language from a mile away.

What a waste of time.

I turned back around in my seat, conflicted. It was an epic internal battle between the encouragement from Mrs. Allen, and the discouragement from my friends. Which would win?

I slowly raised my hand.

"*Dude*," one of my buddies said. "You don't seriously want to do *that*?"

I felt the full force of the judgement of my friends.

Student Council? Trying hard?

Not cool at all, man.

"It actually sounds kind of fun," I said quietly.

But I felt about two feet tall.

That's when the light of Mrs. Allen came into the picture, bubbly, positive, full of enthusiasm, a bright smile on her face.

"*I* think that's a great decision, Jordan!" And then louder, so the class could clearly hear it, she said something that would change how I thought of myself forever: "you are a natural leader."

A natural leader. I liked the idea of that. We were all in sixth grade, dumb preteen boys. I had simply raised my hand to join student council, an introductory exercise in leadership that didn't really change all that much within the greater educational system, and yet, this small little moment changed everything for me.

You are a natural leader.

I had never considered myself a leader. Yet Mrs. Allen illuminated something in me that I had not been able to see before. She believed in me, and it was a belief that grew, and became something real and tangible for me. In front of

Mrs. Allen was a kid, who like every other sixth-grade boy, was being torn down a lot by his peers, but wanted to believe in himself. She had the foresight to see that I had leadership qualities within me, I just needed some illuminating encouragement to develop them.

This moment is really where my leadership journey began. It was my very first opportunity to lead. In middle school and high school, student council gave me a platform to be a leader, to represent my school. I ended up running for high school class president, and even through college and beyond, I continued to gravitate toward leadership roles.

Today, I get to do what I love every single day—be a leader. I get to coach promising athletes and coaches and CEOs and deposit that same, encouraging belief in each of them that Mrs. Allen deposited in me—*you're a natural leader.*

Where Coach Bickford, whom we talked about in Chapter 6, was fanning a flame that already existed, Mrs. Allen was striking a match in an area of my life that was yet to light up.

Jon Gordon, my mentor and friend, often shares that leadership is a transfer of energy and belief. In my life story, Coach Bickford transferred energy—Mrs. Allen transferred belief. Something that Jon Gordon always asks his podcast guests is "When did you first see yourself as a leader?" If someone were to ask me that today, without reservation I could point to the moment that Mrs. Allen called me a leader. What's remarkable about this principle of illumination is that we might not ever know that we've done it. Mrs. Allen probably has no idea how that moment in sixth grade impacted me; I haven't talked to her in years. And yet with just *one single sentence*, she changed my life.

The Art of Illuminating Encouragement

That moment, some several decades ago, was a catalyst moment that had a cascading effect over the rest of my life journey. We often fail to realize just how much others need us to light up their qualities and attributes so they can see them more clearly. We truly never know when something we say might impact someone's life journey, for better or for worse. You have the ability to cast vision for others.

We're all just moments away from being the best version of ourselves.

Everyone around us is moments away from their best life, as well.

They just need someone to believe in them.

When Others See What We Can't

Oftentimes, we need people to help us see what we can't see ourselves. This is the main principle to the art of illumination. What was dark and obscure becomes bright and defined.

There's a quote by Tom Landry, an American football player and former coach of the Dallas Cowboys, who is considered one of the greatest coaches of all time:

"A coach is someone who tells you what you don't want to hear, who has you see what you don't want to see, so you can be who you have always known you could be."

And this is the heart of this chapter, the heart of my vision for what's possible. We are all so capable of so much. Many of us want to try something hard, or something new, we just need someone to encourage us and make us feel like we are up to the task. We all have our version of stepping out of our comfort zone to join the student council.

When we can help others see what they can't see on their own, our belief in them can launch their vision—big or small.

In some ways, we are like kindling, and we can become a roaring fire when someone else lights the match and gives us a confidence we couldn't have had without their encouragement. God gave us the ability to do this for each other. With His wisdom, we can find the right words to support and light others up.

Truly, we are always one moment away from a different life. If it wasn't for Mrs. Allen, I wouldn't have run for student council. If I didn't become class president, I wouldn't have had the confidence to speak in front of other people. And if I didn't have the confidence to speak in front of other people, I wouldn't have started a speaking and leadership company, coaching professional athletes, executive leaders, and high-level sales professionals. I wouldn't be doing what I love.

Vision Casting

At the center of all of this is a simple concept: vision casting.

Casting a vision for someone is like pointing a spotlight on what they can accomplish.

Andy Stanley, the founder and pastor of North Point Ministries, has said one of my favorite quotes:

> "Everyone ends up somewhere in life, very few people end up there on purpose."

The Art of Illuminating Encouragement

This is similar to something I believe in that I call the Law of Drift—without a vision and a path forward, you're drifting.

And no one ever drifted to a destination they intended to be at.

We have to move purposefully and take charge in order to move toward our goals. But this isn't our natural tendency. Instead, most of us drift. It is the path of least resistance. We tend to waste time doubting ourselves. We frequently get stuck in indecision or scared away by the possibility of failure (or our fellow sixth-grade classmates).

Casting a vision is a way to help people arrive at a destination they could maybe not have imagined for themselves. It's a catalyst for driving action, helping people live without regret of the things they wanted to try but were too afraid to.

Vision helps people arrive at their life on purpose.

We can cast a vision about anything, big or small.

It could be helping someone believe they are capable of making the team, giving them the courage they need to try out. Or perhaps it is helping someone see that they could run the business they've always dreamed of, that they could create their own startup from scratch. Sometimes it is as simple as you describing what you think someone is capable of, or encouraging them to reach for a goal that scares them.

At the end of the day, casting vision is about helping people live in the land of possibilities.

Because I don't want them to *think* that they can achieve something.

I want them to *know* it, achieve it.

I want to be the illuminating spark that starts the roaring fire.

James Clear, author of the book *Atomic Habits*, speaks about the act of casting votes for yourself. Within the context of habits, for example, when you go to the gym, you cast a vote for yourself. That vote is in favor of the identity of:

I'm a person who works out.

To me, casting vision for people is like helping them cast votes for their own identity, helping pull them closer to the destiny version of themselves and creating guardrails to help them avoid things that are not true to who they really are.

This chapter, "The Art of Illuminating Encouragement," is about one thing: believing in other people.

And to me, the art of illumination isn't something you fall into by accident; you have to end up there on purpose. You need to intentionally *choose* to see the good, amplify the good, and project the good in others.

We live in a negative world. A world that is mired with people tearing others down and pointing out the worst in them. The universe of social media has allowed us to become bullies from the safety of our own home. Without having to face the consequences of our words, we can make other people out to be monsters, villains, and strangers. There is judgement and strife all around us.

But we are all more alike than not. We are all human, created in the image of God. We are all worthy, and simultaneously completely undeserving. And most of us are all capable of doing so much more with the gifts we've been given; we just need a little help illuminating them.

The Art of Illuminating Encouragement

John Maxwell, American author, speaker, and pastor, and my personal mentor and friend, does something really powerful during his speeches. He will stop, look around at the crowd and simply say:

"I value you."

And of course, the natural reaction from members in the audience is to say: "John, how can you value me? You don't even know *me*."

To which John responds, "You're right. I don't know you. But God created you. And I value what God created."

You can value everyone like that, it's simply a choice to do so.

One of the greatest gifts that we can give to the world while we are in it is to embrace the people who were there for us by, hopefully, paying it forward.

I am so fortunate that I have had so many people in my life believe in me, even when it might not have been easy to do so.

There were days I wasn't fun to be around.

There were days I wasn't the best teammate.

There were 250 days over a school year that I was a sixth-grade boy.

And yet there were people in my life like Mrs. Allen who saw what I couldn't and shone a spotlight on it for me.

So now it is my goal to pay it forward, and shine a light in the lives of those who feel unworthy. I want to be the person who casts a vision and starts people on the trajectory of their real, better futures.

Leading Up in Our Illuminating Encouragement

One thing that I think we often make the mistake of in our encouragement is thinking that those who are in leadership positions above us have it all figured out and don't need our support. Can I let you in on a little secret? Leaders still need encouragement. Leaders still have characteristics and qualities hidden away in the dark that need a little illumination. When we think about leadership, or encouragement in general, it is easy to think about it horizontally, or top down, where we encourage our peers or the team members who report to us. It isn't very often that we think about the person in a position of authority.

A lot of the companies I work with are large corporations, and a CEO might have as many as 100 or more people reporting to them. I often ask the leaders at these companies—"how many people reach out to encourage you each year?" The number of leaders in these companies that have even one person reach out to them in this way is shockingly low.

Don't forget to encourage your boss or your CEO. The "forgotten crowd" is often the leader, manager, boss. They do it for everyone else, but often don't have anyone encouraging them. The biggest myth in leadership is that you have to be in charge to lead. You don't have to have influence to encourage, and you don't have to be in charge to encourage. You can be the least experienced person on your team and still be a leader in encouragement. It's free, it doesn't require experience, it doesn't require you to be a subject matter expert, and it is a simple thing you can do to have big impact.

Does it feel intimidating to you to imagine illuminating a hidden quality or attribute in someone who is in an authority position over you? It shouldn't! If they are a good leader, they will likely really appreciate you shining a light for them!

One of the best examples I have in my own life of this sort of leading up encouragement came from one of my closest friends, Adam Corpstein. I hired Adam a decade ago when I worked for the financial firm. At the time, he was a college student, working for us as an intern. He was different. He had a unique level of charisma and seemed to have boundless levels of energy and enthusiasm. He was, in fact, an enthusiast— excited about almost everything. He quickly grew in the financial planning world, studied for tests, asked questions, showed up early, stayed late. I knew he was going to be special. We grew close quickly.

Adam did something different than the rest of the interns, new hires, and young professionals in the office. I appreciated each newer advisor in our office, but I noticed early on that Adam deeply grasped the Art of Encouragement, and more specifically, that he displayed the power of illumination. I often observed Adam encouraging and casting a vision for his peers and fellow interns. I also noticed how he treated his mentors, like me. He wanted to talk about *my* future, *my* goals, sometimes dreaming with me: "imagine where you will be five years from now."

Adam always seemed to have a knack for getting me to think about the future, and always in a more abundant and positive way. He frequently shone a spotlight on possibilities I had never considered myself. This was never truer than when I got fired. Adam was one of my first phone calls; I had to let him know. It was an uncomfortable situation for me. Here I was telling a dear friend, whom I felt a responsibility to lead, that I had failed and made a mistake.

But Adam only encouraged me.

"This doesn't change anything about your gifts, man, or my level of respect for you" Adam said. "One day this will all make sense. Maybe you will write a book about what you've been through. It will be great; you'll impact and help a bunch of people."

"Write a book?" I laughed a little. "Yes," I said, "maybe one day, I'll write a book."

It felt like light-years away.

"Life moves fast," Adam encouraged me, "I think we will work together again in the future; I really believe that, man. Heck, maybe we'll even live next to each other someday."

Here I am writing a book—an idea that Adam shown a spotlight on all of those years ago. Today, Adam is a part of our coaching team at Montgomery Companies. He just moved into his new home with his wife Emily, just a few streets away from Ashley and me. Life is good, and Adam was right—it moves fast. He breathed some life into these pages. The power of illumination.

Reader Challenge

In this chapter, we learned about how we can cast a vision for others, illuminate something about themselves that they might not have seen otherwise. Mrs. Allen did that for me when she showed me that I was a natural leader—she highlighted an innate trait that I didn't know I had until she created a way, through student council, for me to display it.

This week, I want you to light a match for each of your 10 encouragees. This will require you to really put some time and energy into thinking about the person, because you are illuminating something that they may not even see about themselves. Unlike the previous challenge, where you were encouraging your people about something they do and making them feel like they are the best at it, in this challenge, you are encouraging them about something that may be hidden beneath the surface. What traits and characteristics can you find in your encouragees that they might not be fully aware of?

The practical way to do this is to speak one thing into existence for each of the 10 people you are encouraging. If you completed the art of care challenge in Chapter 5, then you should have a sense of their goals, desires, and wishes. The key in *this* challenge is to give them a vision that is grander than what they could imagine for themselves. Mrs. Allen tapped into a desire she could see was in my heart—a desire to be a leader—that I didn't think was possible, and she lit a match.

This type of encouragement might not be exactly your style, and that's okay! This is just an exercise to get the gears turning. You do you, and be authentic to who you are, or the encouragement won't feel genuine.

Write down your observations from doing this exercise in the space allotted for Chapter 7 in the back of the book. What qualities and characteristics did you discover in your encouragee during this challenge? Did you notice new things about this person that you had never seen before? How did the encouragee respond to this type of encouragement? How did you feel during and after the conversation with them? As always, write it all down!

Chapter 8

The Art of Elevating Encouragement

One of my favorite forms of encouragement is the art of elevation. There is nothing I love more than shouting someone's praise into the proverbial megaphone. When we elevate someone, we help them get the recognition they deserve, often through making strategic introductions to create new opportunities and endorse them publicly.

As a public speaker, I literally have a stage to stand on and sing people's praises from. But the art of elevating someone—making much of their success, promoting them, spotlighting them, giving them public praise, helping them get recognized—does not require a stage. When you help connect someone and expand their circle, advocating for them and increasing awareness of how awesome they are, you are practicing the art of elevation. It could be as simple as introducing them to someone you think might benefit from their services, or writing a review for a small business owner online, endorsing them on LinkedIn, talking about them in a social media post, or nominating them for an award.

When you elevate people—you give them their most basic, relational need—to be seen, heard, and known. By helping to promote them, you push them out and prop them up. You highlight their God-given talents in front of others, encouraging them to step even further into those gifts and grow in their potential. You encourage them to go further than they thought they could.

God works through people. He uses us to help others, to encourage them. And one incredibly powerful way to do that is to elevate someone in front of others. It is a public display of appreciation and belief, in which we get to tell them how wonderful they are and how much they mean to us.

There's a phenomenon that happens when people praise you in public. A private endorsement is wonderful, but for some reason, in public the impact of that endorsement is multiplied. A moment is created.

Like many of the greatest things in this life, the Art of Elevating Encouragement doesn't have to be complicated to be effective. We all want to feel valued, and when someone compliments us or calls us out for an accomplishment, or even just acknowledges us in public, it shows us that our efforts haven't gone unnoticed. That we are known. It's like someone saying:

Hey, I see you.

I notice you.

You matter.

We can be the ultimate connector and promotor of others. We can be the reason people win more, feel better, get a promotion at work, get noticed, or meet their future spouse. We can be the reason people have more opportunities, achieve more, and feel better.

Just about everyone we know is fighting a battle we know nothing about, and you can be a light in whatever they are walking through.

When it comes to business, many of us understand the power of marketing. We understand how important it is to highlight a product, tout its features, get buy-in for what we are selling. We see billboards and advertisements, and we know that companies are spending millions on promotion. Yet we spend very little time thinking about or putting effort behind marketing our people—elevating and promoting our friends, peers, coworkers, and family. Elevating others is one of the fastest ways to improve our work culture, improve performance, and improve both our lives and the lives of those around us.

So how can you start practicing this art today? Anytime you have the chance, anytime you have the proverbial megaphone, be the one who lifts someone up. In that moment, point out the good in them. Dote on the qualities that you love about them. Brag about them.

Even those not directly being encouraged will feel the positivity that radiates from this type of encouragement! In our chapter on authenticity (Chapter 10), we talk about the importance of leading in our vulnerability. I firmly believe that it shows a vulnerability to highlight someone else, especially in front of a crowd. In this way, it demonstrates authenticity that is attractive and trustworthy, so you get to practice two arts for the price of one!

The Art of Elevating Encouragement

There is something moving and powerful about using your own moment in the spotlight to give credit and praise to others in the room. It is backward of what many expect, so it catches them by surprise, which immediately draws them in and brings them to the edge of their seats. You'll notice that a lot of the great orators do this—they're constantly directing the spotlight on other people. They use every opportunity they can to elevate.

It is one of my favorite things to do when I give a keynote. As part of my prep work, I'll ask for the names of five people who will be in the audience. I don't want the top performers. I want the people in the organization that might be undervalued, but hold their teams together. When the day of the speech comes, I start highlighting everything great I've been told about these five people. Inevitably it is in this part of the speech that everyone claps and cheers, bringing a wave of gratitude and grace. It is meaningful to those getting the encouragement, but also to everyone around them, too.

Going Up! The Natural Elevator

Have you ever been around someone who just naturally knows how to elevate you? Simply being in their presence gives you more opportunity, more hope, more optimism.

I'm fortunate that I have had many friends who have done this for me over the years, but there is one person who does this better than anyone I have ever known, who also happens to be one of my best friends. His name is David Nurse, and he is the ultimate elevator of people. To know David is to know 100 new friends. He will open 100 new doors, make 100 new connections, and find 100 ways to elevate you. He has made it his life's mission to elevate people.

I get a voice text or phone call from David approximately once every other day, if not daily. The mission of every message is the same: to add value, to elevate. "Hey Jordan, just thinking of you, brother; I want to connect you with this person . . ." "Jordan I have an amazing idea for you . . ." "Jordan, I have to invite you to this upcoming event!" For David, it's just become a part of who he is. It's organic, potent, and real.

David is originally from the great state of Iowa, but his work has taken him all over the globe. He is a former NBA shooting coach, turned speaker, author, and entrepreneur. When I was first getting to know David, I invited him to some of my events in Iowa, as he had a book coming out, and after following his work for a while I knew it would be an ideal time for him to tour and speak. I admired David, and I wanted to help promote his new book, add value to his work, and develop a meaningful relationship with him.

A few short months later, we had our first opportunity to meet in Iowa. I invited him to dinner at one of my favorite restaurants. I arrived at the restaurant early, so that I could be prepared and ready to be a great host. The goal of the visit was really about promoting his new book, which I knew was very important to him, and I wanted to make sure the whole world knew about it (or at least all of Iowa!).

When David arrived, he greeted me as if I was a long-time best friend whom he hadn't seen in forever.

The Art of Elevating Encouragement

"Jordan!!! Man, it is SO good to see you! I'm so thrilled to be here with you in Iowa!"

We had never met in person before that moment, but he sure didn't make it feel that way. Over the next 24 hours, David asked more questions and handed out more compliments than anyone I have ever met. And he didn't just do this for me, he did it for everyone! Literally *everyone* he met. At multiple points, I thought to myself, *no one can be this nice, right? What is his deal?* I thought there might be a catch—no one could really be this serious about adding value without looking for something in return.

But I am happy to share that many years and a best friendship later, I have learned that amazingly, David Nurse really *is* that nice. He is one of the most caring, kind, and generous people I've ever met. God put him on this earth to elevate people.

Indirectly, David has connected me to some of the greatest thought leaders I know, literally dozens of leaders! And because he has connected me to amazing leaders like Brad Lomenick, I've connected to hundreds of leaders. Brad is truly one of the most gifted connectors on the planet. Brad has connected me to hundreds of leaders, speakers, coaches, authors, pastors, many who have been 100% formative in my own leadership journey. I have Brad to thank for many of my closest friends and mentoring relationships. Close friends like Chad Johnson and Ryan Leak, and mentoring relationships with leaders like John Maxwell and Patrick Lencioni. It has been extremely encouraging to me to have this list of mentors in my journey for growth, and that encouragement comes courtesy of Brad and David.

For natural elevators like David and Brad, the formula is simple. So simple that I've been able to pick up on it over the years: ask more questions than everyone else, see the good in people, point it out to others, and then find ways to help those people. This formula has worked for David and Brad in incredible ways. They are people magnets, a living, breathing furnace of human connection.

And you can be, too, by walking out the art of elevation.

Reader Challenge

For your encouragees, nothing is more encouraging than being elevated in a way that furthers their own God-given missions. For this challenge, I want you to think about how you can connect, promote, endorse, and advertise your encouragees.

Do you know someone that you think might really mesh well with one of your encouragees? Introduce them! Is your encouragee looking to get into a new line of work? Connect them with someone in that industry! Think of ways that you can endorse and promote that individual publicly, and shout into the proverbial megaphone about how awesome they are. You will have to work within your own means of course, but as I mentioned earlier in the chapter, it could be as simple as introducing them to someone you think might benefit from their services, or writing a review for a small business owner online, endorsing them on LinkedIn, talking about them in a social media post, or nominating them for an award.

Write down your observations in the Chapter 8 Observations section at the back of the book. How were you able to elevate your encouragees, and what form did the elevation take? How did they respond? How did you feel doing it? What good things do you see coming from these new connections? Record it all!

Chapter 9

The Art of Serving Encouragement

A s the host of the *Growth Over Goals* podcast, I've had the tremendous opportunity to interview and glean wisdom from many great thought leaders. A year or so ago, I was interviewing my friend Patrick Lencioni, founder of the Table Group, on the podcast, and the topic of "servant leadership" came up. He shared how much he dislikes the term, because in his mind, you are not truly leading if you are not serving. To him, the two terms are inseparable—servant leadership isn't a *type* of leadership, it is the *definition* of leadership!

Fundamentally, if you think about the historical leaders we truly respect—Jesus Christ, Mother Teresa, Gandhi, Nelson Mandela, Martin Luther King Jr.—what they all have in common was this: they put others before themselves. They lived in the spirit of service. They didn't think about what they could get out of others. They didn't only help those that could help them. They were people who believed in self-sacrifice, in doing for others, and they did it fully.

I've often thought about that idea since that conversation, and after reflecting on my own leadership journey and the journeys of those that I've coached, I must say I couldn't agree more. One of the greatest ways to encourage someone is to offer your talents and skills in service to them. Make their goals your goals, and their agenda your agenda. This chapter will give you the tools you need to do just that. So, let's dive in!

Making the Leader's Agenda Your Agenda

Every single one of the guests I have interviewed on the *Growth Over Goals* podcast has proven to be incredibly formative in my own personal leadership and coaching journey, but there was one podcast guest in particular that transformed the way I saw the art of service and how it pertains to encouragement. That guest was Mark Cole.

Mark Cole is the CEO of Maxwell Leadership enterprises. He has an incredible 25 years of leadership and team development experience and has helped countless companies grow and improve through various challenges and disconnected team dynamics. He's worked with John C. Maxwell for years and has had the chance to work with some of the most impactful leaders to ever walk the planet. I could not wait to hear how Mark's perspective on leadership and influence was shaped by these interactions.

I concluded the podcast interview with Mark like every other, by asking him one of my favorite questions: "What advice would you give to emerging leaders who want to grow in their influence?"

Mark's answer was simple, but powerful:

"Find out what the leader's agenda is," he said. "And make that your agenda for a season."

Mark went on to explain that for the last 20 years he has made it his mission to serve others, and in the process of doing so has watched his career and his influence flourish. Mark shared that true growth, achievement, and impact were less about "knowing the right people" and more about coming humbly alongside those people in a way that enabled you to make their agenda your agenda. By offering yourself in this posture of service, you would honor and encourage others, helping them walk in their own God-given giftedness and elevating their mission above your own, even if only for a season.

After the podcast, I couldn't get those words out of my head. There were so many leaders I looked up to that I would give anything to learn from. Could it really be as easy as making their agenda mine and serving just to serve? Would that really change anything? I was willing to try.

But who? Who could I serve and provide value to?

I spent time carefully thinking and praying about the decision before I decided to reach out to Jon Gordon. Jon Gordon is one of the most influential leadership authors and speakers across the nation. He's a consultant to a number of high-level executive leaders in the boardroom, on the football field and basketball courts, coaching CEOs as well as NFL, NBA, and MLB coaches, championship teams and high performers. Jon is an inspirational teacher who has helped millions of people have a more positive mindset. I respected him as an author and a speaker, and I trusted him. Our values were deeply aligned, and I admired him.

Jon had been a guest on my podcast before, and we'd connected here and there, so I figured a call to him wouldn't be totally out of the blue.

The Art of Serving Encouragement

I tried not to overthink it.

"Look," I said, getting right to the point. "I recently inter-viewed Mark Cole on my podcast, and he spoke about how to expand your influence and grow as a leader, and what he said to me—it was really thought-provoking. He told me to *"Make the leader's agenda your agenda for a season"*—and a lightbulb went off for me. Jon, I'd love to do that with you. I know there are some things you care about that I would love an opportu-nity to help you with. I don't expect you to respond right this moment, and I don't need anything in return, but if I can serve you for this year, you can count me in."

Jon was silent for a moment. I could tell he was surprised by my offer.

And no wonder. It's not often that someone reaches out with no agenda of their own besides to serve someone else's (again, credit Mark Cole, this was *not* my bright idea). All too often we are focused on what we get out of our ser-vice to others, asking ourselves, how can helping this person benefit me?

But have you ever considered flipping that on its head? Serving just to serve? Making their agenda yours?

People expect complicated solutions to growing in your influence and leadership, but so often the magic is in the sim-ple and unexpected answers. That was certainly true of my time with Jon.

Jon gladly accepted my offer, and as I started down the path of serving his agenda, a transformation in my own life began.

The work wasn't profound. I helped Jon throw a few events, planning the logistics and working with his team, organizing dinners the night before, inviting people to the dinner, figuring out who would support the event, and trying to find the right restaurant venue that would work with the clientele. I posted on my own social media, sharing his events, and started advocacy outreach, recruiting people, making phone calls and sending emails trying to find sponsors. In other words, I helped Jon and his team make things happen. I simply served. I wasn't being paid for the work, I just wanted to learn from Jon and help him in this season. I wanted to see if this kind of generosity would spur the personal growth and bring about a new level of trust and relationship that Mark Cole had suggested.

And it did. It really, really did.

Because after a time of serving Jon and being completely invested in his agenda, Jon began to invest in me.

After hosting a successful event for Jon in my backyard in Iowa, we packed up and headed out to take Jon to the airport. We debriefed about the day, both happy with how things had gone. After a bit of conversation Jon paused. He looked at me and asked, "So, Jordan, what else can we do together?"

"What else are you thinking about, Jon?" I asked him. "How else can I add value?"

Jon is one of those visionaries who always has a lot of irons in the fire. There is no shortage of projects brewing in his mind. We talked through some of his ideas, and I offered to help bring them to life.

"If I could help you pour some more gas on that fire, Jon, I'm there. I want to be helpful."

"Man . . . I don't know," he said, thinking. He seemed grateful, but a little perplexed. "This is just awesome of you, but don't you want anything out of this? I want to make sure I'm helping you. How do I take care of you?"

Little did he know, of course, that his dedicated mentorship, spending time with him and gleaning from his wealth of experience, wisdom, and faith, was one of the most valuable gifts I'd ever received in my own career. It was, in many ways, priceless. I was well aware that a number of people would give large sums of money to spend the kind of time I was spending with Jon.

I looked at Jon, recalling the conversation we'd first had earlier that year.

"I told you I would serve. I value your mentorship. You're teaching me a lot. If I'm trying to 'get' something out it—it kind of diminishes my service. I'm open to future conversations . . ." These future conversations have led to Jon being very generous.

He looked back to me, reassuringly.

"Look," he said. "I'm all in on you. Anything to help you grow."

Hearing those words from somebody I had admired for years was everything I needed.

Mark Cole was right. Totally and completely right.

The Spirit of Service

John C. Maxwell often speaks about the difference between success and significance. As he puts it, you can have a lot of success, but that does not necessarily make you significant. Rather, the people who are remembered as the most significant are the people who are remembered as giving themselves in service to the world. Those are the people we remember and revere, the people we still talk about hundreds and thousands of years later.

"The greatest among you shall be your servant. For whoever exalts himself will be humbled, and whoever humbles himself will be exalted."

Matthew 23:11-12.

"But among you it will be different. Whoever wants to be a leader among you must be your servant."

Matthew 20:26

These scriptures from our greatest Teacher and Leader set the example for us to follow. Being generous with no expectation of receiving anything in return, doing more than you have to and not keeping score—that is how you truly lead a life of significance and exemplify leadership.

When you serve, it encourages the people around you. A servant's heart sets you apart from the crowd. Instead of being yet another person asking for something, you become different, you become a source of selfless love and encouragement.

And it turns out, as I learned during my season of serving Jon, that level of serving usually makes them want to help and invest in you, too.

I understand that some people might want to argue this point. As businesspeople, it is a simple fact that we do need help from others and value in return for our service. But I would challenge you to view your acts of service differently.

The Art of Serving Encouragement

As my friend—renowned expert in the field of business and team management—Pat Lencioni, says "The personal economics don't have to make sense."

Stop focusing on the personal economics for a season and see how your influence changes and grows. What you'll find is when the personal economics don't make sense, when you're not keeping score, when you're focused on bringing value without any strings attached, that's usually when you receive the most value in return.

Mike O'Connell, pastor of Love Church, and former co-captain of the Iowa State football team, is a perfect example of this principle in motion. Unless you are deep within the world of college football, you might not know Mike, and that's how he prefers it. Mike is one of the most gifted communicators I have ever known, but he isn't one to seek fame; quite the opposite really. Mike's life mission and passion is helping others feel known.

As long as I have known Mike, he's been like this. In college on the Iowa State football team, where he was known as the ultimate teammate, Mike went from a non-scholarship walk-on to a three-year starter and was voted a team captain his senior season, an accomplishment he remained completely humble about. After college, Mike began an extremely successful career in medical sales, but finding the job lacking in a purpose-driven mission, left his six-figure salary and moved to Omaha, Nebraska, to work at a church in an entry-level staff position. This career transition, from Division One athlete, to successful businessman, to serving a church as a lower-level staff member, was not exactly what one would call "climbing the ladder," but everything about the way Mike operates is backward in the world's eyes.

Through his work at the church, Mike eventually found his calling behind the microphone, sharing and preaching in small settings, and today he preaches the word at one of the largest churches in Omaha on a regular basis. Several years ago, Mike attended one of our Montgomery Companies leadership events. Although an extremely gifted speaker himself at that point, Mike simply wanted to come hang out as an attendee—"I will be in the area, and it will be a great opportunity for me to learn," he told me.

I was thrilled to have Mike there. Mike is an asset to every room that he is in, and I knew it would be a major win to have him present at this event. But even I wasn't prepared for his incredible level of service. Without being asked, Mike showed up early to help unpack the truck and set up the venue, he stayed late to help us break down and clean up, he engaged with our team and the event attendees throughout the day and made himself available for whatever was needed. Without any sort of agenda of his own, Mike served.

Here is what makes all of this more interesting—this was an event that featured several speakers. Mike wasn't speaking that day, but he was the most talented speaker in the room. He chose not to speak. He chose to carry boxes, set up, clean up. He took notes as the speakers were talking. He encouraged the speakers afterwards . . . "I learned a ton from you today, thanks for the powerful message!" This was the Mike I knew and loved. To me, Mike represents the most important quality in servant leadership—humility.

The art of service begins by dying to self. Service always requires us to give something away—our time, our energy, our

The Art of Serving Encouragement

money, our own wants and needs, sometimes even our own best interest. It requires us to offer up all of who we are and expect nothing in return.

The economics of this level of servant-minded exchange, while not straightforward, *are* often interesting. I love how Bob Burg, Hall of Fame speaker and best-selling coauthor of The Go-Giver book series, communicates about this kind of spending. He points out that in the economics of human interaction, spending does not deplete, it multiplies. The more support you give away, the more you have. And the same is true with attention, empathy, counsel, etc.

Bob is right! One of my favorite quotes of his is: "Your true worth is determined by how much more you give in value than you take in payment." I couldn't agree more. Understanding that single principle has dramatically altered the way that I approach life and business, looking at every interaction as an opportunity to give, serve, love, and encourage. That is the art of service. A humble approach to adding value and not keeping track of the score!

The Service of Time

Out of all the things we can give in this world, the hardest thing to give (and the most valuable thing to give) is our time. I think of time as a resource much like money, or material possessions, and one of the best ways to encourage others is with your time, prioritizing people in key moments.

As I've said before in this book—love and encouragement are spelled T-I-M-E.

Over the past two years, a friend of mine, Dale Mullikin, has met up with me almost every other week. We study the Bible together and have wonderful conversations about parenting, marriage, God, and life in general.

One day, I said to Dale, "Dale, you've met with me for over a year now, and sometimes, I feel like a burden. I'm not paying you. I call on you to just help me out with things, and you're just always there for me."

Dale's response exemplified servant leadership:

"Jesus said go forth and make disciples," he said. "I'm called to this work. That's why I do it."

I was caught off guard by just how different that is than how most people view service to others. In a world where everybody is trying to get something, want something, be somebody, have something, go somewhere, make "something" happen, this version of truly altruistic service is so rare.

Dale's service in this season of my life has been an unspeakable encouragement to me.

Service is, I believe, the highest form of belief and generosity. When people give out of love, authentic care, and genuine support you can feel it, and it makes all the difference. I've felt it from Dale, I've felt it from Jon, and I've benefited tremendously from this incredible form of encouragement.

And yet so many of our relationships at work, in our communities, and at home, are focused on our own personal agendas. We provide service and encouragement only in times when the return on our investment is clear.

But what would your leadership look like if you focused on serving others just to serve them?

109

The Art of Serving Encouragement

How would your influence grow?

What impact could you truly make?

I have one person in my life who has excelled in the encouraging art of service for me with a different type of cadence and a unique level of consistency. He has been there for nearly every meaningful event or happening in my life since childhood. He shows up when things are planned long in advance. He shows up on short notice. He shows up spur of the moment. Heck, he has even shown up a time or two when I didn't want him to. If it's an important event in my life, you can be sure this friend will be there.

His name is Travis Kern. He's been my best friend since childhood and in our younger years we were joined at the hip. Most of my fondest memories of childhood include Travis. As I grew older, it felt odd to experience meaningful moments without Travis present. Of course, as the years passed and our lives evolved, it became impossible to spend the same amount of time together. We went off to college, got married, had children, and devoted more time to our careers. But though a lot of life has occurred since our childhood days, and so much has changed, there is one thing that hasn't changed—Travis's willingness to give the service of his time freely. Whenever I need someone to be there for me, Travis is there, no questions asked. He doesn't need to know why. He just needs to know that I need him. Travis has taught me an incredibly important lesson about the art of encouragement, that one of our most encouraging assets is the gift of our time.

Perhaps this depth of involvement in your coworkers', friends', or family's lives feels unrealistic to you. I get it, life is busy! The goal is not to be omnipresent. The goal is to make it matter when it matters most, to serve others in the ways that bless them the most. Sometimes this means being there for a supportive conversation when the person is going through a hard time, and sometimes it simply means showing up for them on important occasions. Regardless of the reason or the need, the greatest gift you can give those that you care about is the service of your time.

I would love to tell you that I have always operated with this kind of service, that I have been the friend or family member who has always been there for others when it mattered most. Unfortunately, I have actually failed at this many times.

Most recently, I found myself sitting in the Chicago airport with tears rolling down my face as I spoke on the phone with my daughter, Audrey. Against my better judgement, I said yes to a speaking engagement on the East Coast the day before her birthday. I knew when I said yes to this event that I had very little margin for error, as I would be returning late afternoon the day of Audrey's birthday. Sure enough, my flight got delayed. I sat on a bench in the Chicago airport, Facetiming my daughter, and had to explain that I wouldn't make it home that night. By choosing to contract the speaking engagement, I missed the opportunity to show up for my daughter on one of the most important days of her year.

The following day, after returning home, I picked Audrey up from her dance class. I was eager to see her, although admittedly I felt sheepish confronting the fact that I missed her birthday. I gave her a big hug and made some comments about how lousy I felt to have failed to be there for her. After a few short moments of banter, I inquired about her birthday.

"So, how was the big day, Sis?"

"Really good," she responded.

"Best one yet?" I pressed.

"No, not the best one yet . . . you weren't there," she remarked.

I was completely devastated. I decided then and there that I would never feel this way again, and I made a commitment to never miss an important event for my children again. I committed to serve my family in love.

Life is short. Let's give those we love the most the best asset we have—the service of our time and energy.

Serving Well

So how do we serve well? Where does one even start?

These are common questions I encounter when I encourage people to enter into a mindset of serving and giving.

The most important principle is knowing *who* to serve. This is one of the most crucial questions to ask yourself, because when you choose an individual or organization to serve, you will make their agenda your agenda. It goes without saying that you don't want to ally yourself with a person or organization that isn't centered on the foundations of good moral values, such as integrity, honesty, truth, justice, love, etc. It's important that the agenda you are serving is one that aligns with your own core values and internal mission statement. It should be something or someone that you feel excited about giving your time and energy to. For me, that person was Jon Gordon, a man of integrity and purpose, whom I knew I could wholeheartedly serve without reservation.

Don't know where to begin? Start by asking yourself some key questions; such as, what is your internal mission statement? How do you want to give yourself in service to the world? Do you have a passion for sales? Or health? Or charitable works? Do you want to become a CEO? A pastor? A stay-at-home parent? A teacher? These are just a few examples of admirable life missions, but the possibilities are endless!

Once you know what it is you want to do, even if it is just for a season, find someone who you believe does it well. Look for someone who you feel has been extremely successful in the field you want to serve in, and reach out to them to ask them how you can help them. This may feel intimidating, but what is there for you to lose? The worst that can happen is that they'll say no to your offer to serve their agenda, and I can tell you right now based on my own experience, you will be surprised at how often people—even busy, successful, important people—say yes.

Once you know *who* you want to serve, the crux of service becomes dependent on understanding *what* you can offer to someone that adds value to their world. You need to know first-hand what is important to the individual, their organization, and their family. Everyone is different and needs different things, so seek to understand first.

The best way to gain this information is to simply ask. Be curious. Ask questions. Go beyond the normal sense of inquiry, like I shared in the example with Jon Gordon earlier in this chapter.

I have a great rule that you can follow when you are seeking out this level of information from someone you want to serve:

To be a good question asker, ask a second question.

A second question is one that brings more depth to the information you just received by asking your first question. I will demonstrate how this works in the following two different scenarios—one in which a second question was not utilized, and one in which it was.

For example, for scenario one, let's say you're chatting with a new friend, and you are getting to know them. We'll call this friend "Jeff."

"Jeff, do you have a favorite hobby?"

"Yes!" says Jeff, "I'm an artist, I love to paint."

"No way!" you respond. "My grandmother was an artist; I feel like it really inspired my love of art. Just the other day . . ."

That's one way the conversation could go. There is nothing inherently wrong with it; you're making conversation. It is actually a fairly natural and normal response.

But, let's see how it compares to scenario two:

"Jeff, do you have a favorite hobby?"

"Yes!" says Jeff, "I'm an artist, I love to paint."

"No way!" you respond. "Do you have a favorite painting that you've done, and if so, what did you love about it?"

Do you see the difference? When you learn to ask the second (and third, and fourth) question, you start to make a habit of gathering a complete picture of who someone is, what they need, what they want, what they love, and what they are interested in. You can find out all sorts of things with the second question.

In a sense, when you ask the second question, you start to understand where they are, and who they are. When you understand those variables, you can really begin to add value in service to them.

Reader Challenge

In this chapter, the reader challenge will shift a bit, because it would be too great of a commitment to ask you to serve 10 people at once, though I do want you to continue encouraging your 10 people just as you have been from the start as you engage in this exercise.

For this challenge, we will start small. I realize that dedicating your life for a season (whatever that means to you) is a pretty big decision, and it needs to be made thoughtfully and not on impulse. So, for this challenge, we will just give you a taste of what that looks like; I want you to find someone or something you can serve, just for a weekend. Bonus points if it is one of your 10 encouragees, but if there isn't an obvious fit for this exercise within that group, then perhaps it's someone you know from work, or school, or your Bible study group, or your kid's school. Maybe it's your church, or a local soup kitchen, or a family farm. Whoever or whatever it is, reach out to them to ask how you can—again, just for a weekend—serve them. How can you make their agenda your agenda?

Write the name of the person or organization you choose to serve for this exercise in the Chapter 9 observation space in the back of the book. In the Observations section, write down the experiences you have as you serve. What did you learn? How did it feel to make someone else's agenda your agenda? What did you think about serving someone without expecting anything in return? What was the hardest part for you about giving up your time and resources in this way? What was your favorite part? These are just some reflection questions to help you get started with a meaningful response, but journal however and whatever is most impactful to you.

Chapter 10

The Art of Authentic Encouragement

There are two sides to the Art of Authentic Encouragement. One is being an authentic person, and the other is sharing an authentic message. I want to dive into both of these with you in the next few pages, starting with the importance of being an authentic person.

The Art of Being an Authentic Person

A few years into my career as a motivational speaker, I was on my way to a speaking engagement one afternoon when I experienced a transformational moment. As always, I was running through the speech I planned to share over and over again in my mind while soft worship music played in the background.

Out of nowhere, an unexpected thought came to me:

"Am I really sharing what God wants me to share?"

It was a convicting question.

I stopped the internal rehearsal. For the first time in years, I began to revisit my talk, as I questioned whether the content I was planning to share was having the influence I wanted it to have. Was it enough? Was I really glorifying God and all that He had faithfully walked me through? Did it do justice to my trials and the subsequent restoration in my life? Did it highlight what God had done for me?

I began to reflect thoughtfully on my speech, and the opportunity to impact hundreds of people that were before me as a public speaker.

Am I just sharing tactics and strategies?

Or am I sharing something real? Something that God wants me to share?

Something deeper. Something more authentic.

The worship song was still playing in the background of my car, and in that moment, I needed the truths it was pushing me toward.

What if I scrapped my whole speech?

What if I ditched the "perfected" talk and instead went with something a little more raw and off the cuff?

I was simultaneously both excited and scared by the idea. It could be an amazing opportunity. Or, it could be an amazing train wreck.

Minutes away from getting on stage, the thoughts still kept flooding in—good idea, bad idea—back and forth, back and forth.

It was now or never. I had to make a decision.

Okay, God. I prayed. *If you want me to do this—I trust you.*

And then I got on stage.

I saw hundreds of people's eyes looking back at me. Waiting for me to give my polished, public presentation.

But I didn't.

It was a pretty rough start.

"I don't know how I'm going to share this . . . because . . . well, I haven't really talked about this before."

I paused. Deep breath.

Here we go.

"I want to tell you about one of the hardest seasons I have ever experienced in my life," I started. "And it began with what I thought was my dream career."

And so, I launched into the extremely personal, extremely humiliating story of my termination—the same story I opened this book with.

Before I knew it, I could feel the tears welling up in my eyes.

Oh no, this is not good.

I'll spare you the painful details and simply say that I did *not* give that story in a polished, professional way. There were awkward pauses. A lot of them. There were too many "ums" and definitely more tears than I was expecting. I strayed from my usual style of prepared content, and instead of slow and precise words I was fast and hurried. At one point, I stopped talking completely, and lost track of my thoughts. I'd officially entered the zone of a speaker's worst nightmare: disconnected sentences, awkward pauses, and sweating through my suit.

A lot of the time, when you're a professional speaker, you have 90% of the crowd. But I had 100%. Everyone was laser focused on me; probably, I thought to myself, because they were waiting to see how this absolute disaster of a speech would unfold.

I finished the story, and basically pile-drove through the rest of my talk. And then I walked off stage. Silence.

The Art of Authentic Encouragement

The event host quickly hopped up on stage and said a few awkward words of thanks to me before closing things down and dismissing everyone.

I wanted to run away.

That's when my head turned. There was a line of people waiting to talk to me. Usually, after a speech, I have a few people come up to say hi, ask me questions, or talk strategy. It's generally pretty surface level and action oriented.

This was different.

I stopped and greeted each person in turn. Over and over again I heard things like:

"That really touched me . . ."

"I'm actually going through something similar . . ."

"I've battled with sickness and financial strain for years, and . . ."

They kept coming. People with similar stories of hurt and struggle. Each had their own grief, their own story of walking through the valley.

One woman's story in particular really stuck with me.

"My son is ill," she said. "And you don't know how much of an encouragement it was to see your vulnerability."

Here's the deal.

While I hope to never feel as uncomfortable giving a talk as I did that day, I learned one hugely important lesson: the value of authenticity.

People connected with me through my struggle and grief. I could have stood up there and given my polished talk and maybe they would have gained some helpful information from it. But instead, for the first time, I allowed myself to be vulnerable and share an imperfect mess of a message, and it resonated in a deep, meaningful way.

Craig Groeschel, pastor of Life Church and well-known author and speaker, captures this phenomenon perfectly in his teaching with leaders. He says, "People can be impressed by your strengths, but they connect to you through your weaknesses."

I'm not sure about you, but I'd much rather be impactful than impressive. That's not to say I always get it right. I am just as guilty as anyone of spending too much of my life wanting to impress people, wanting to be a perfect picture of what they had imagined, and doing my best to appear polished and professional. But the days when I've had the most impact, where I really felt most in line with my purpose, are the days when I was the most real.

When you allow yourself to be vulnerable, and you let others see that you're not perfect, that you have flaws, that you've made mistakes and walked through hard things, you actually encourage people.

We're all imperfect. We all have issues, flaws, limitations, and hardships. Unfortunately, we tend to compare our insides with everybody else's outside. I know all my insides, all the mental garbage I keep, and all the ways I fall short. And yet with everyone else, I just see the perfect picture, the polished outside. This is greatly and devastatingly compounded by social media, where we are constantly bombarded by an inauthentic image of others' lives as they share only the most perfectly photographed moments, many of which are not even real but were contrived for the sake of the image.

People want to feel connected to those who lead them. And the best way to foster connection, show people you care, that you are real, and that you understand, is through vulnerability.

Leaders, need to be authentic, not perfect. Your willingness to show vulnerability and weakness is actually an incredible superpower. It allows others to be okay with the fact that they're not perfect, either. It helps them see that even with flaws, you can have great impact.

The opposite is also true; when you see someone without a chink in their armor, who seems perfect, it's like a magnifying glass for your own insecurities. You feel like you could never measure up.

At the end of the day, people want to be around the authentic leader. They want to serve the person they can identify with. They want to feel connected to a real person, and know that they are seen and understood. They want someone who has also walked through hard things, who can guide them to use their brokenness, too.

Vulnerability and authenticity are the ultimate encouragers. When people know that you are real, they are encouraged that they are real, too. They feel connected, understood, and ready to lead and excel despite their imperfections.

I'm not saying to share everything you've ever gone through, constantly. There definitely is such a thing as TMI. I probably shared my own story a little too soon. Not all stories are made for everyone, and definitely not all stories are made for the stage. It is good to be judicious about whom to share with, and when.

You don't need to share your deepest, darkest secrets to be authentic and vulnerable. I'm simply challenging you to be okay with sharing things that aren't exclusively positive and polished. Share well, and share tactfully, in a way that feels comfortable for you and the moment.

The Art of Sharing an Authentic Message

There is another side to this type of encouragement that goes beyond being an authentic person, and that is being authentic and specific in choosing your words. I learned this lesson the hard way in my early years of public speaking, from a coach— Bob Teichart—who was wise and bold enough to call me out in a moment where I was being inauthentic.

Bob is old school; he has been coaching people for a long time. He's known for being a truth-teller, and he is pretty direct.

When I finally had a chance to meet him at his conference room, I shook his hand and told him: "Thanks for your time, I'm honored to visit with you. I've heard some awesome things about you."

He looked at me and smiled dimly.

"Oh?" he said. "What have you heard about me?"

And then I thought: *Oh, crap.*

I couldn't think of anything specific.

I floundered. "Oh, you know, some great things about you, people just speak very highly of you."

He looked at me some more.

"And?" he pressed. "What kind of things?"

It was soon apparent that I didn't have all the things I wanted to say. I didn't have anything specific. He piped back in.

"Can I share some feedback?" he said.

"Sure," I said.

He paused.

"I think you're full of it," he said. "And one of the things you need to work on is your sincerity and authenticity."

I looked at him, a little shocked.

"If you're going to say something," he said. "Say something that's specific and believable."

Ouch.

But also, point taken.

I can promise you that I never made that mistake again; I'll have a specific example to support my kind words.

I'm eternally grateful to Bob for helping me grow a tremendous amount in that moment. I've kept his advice to be specific and believable close to my heart for years since, and I can tell you that I am a better encourager because of it.

If you are going to offer encouragement to others, it is important for that encouragement to be authentic. People can smell a phony message from a mile away. I think there is some wisdom to the old adage, "if you can't say anything nice, don't say anything at all," but I would reframe it to say, "if you can't say anything authentic, don't say anything at all."

I wanted to encourage Bob, and my heart was in the right place, but it would have been far better to simply say that I couldn't wait to learn more about him—which was true—than to pretend I already knew something I didn't.

Reader Challenge

Well, dear reader, you have reached your final challenge in this book, but I truly hope you will keep putting into practice the arts you learned in your daily life, with those you regularly interact with.

For this challenge, I would like you to implement, if possible, both of the sides of authenticity you learned here—being vulnerable and real, and sharing a specific and believable message.

If the moment calls for it with one of your encouragees, share something difficult that you have gone through with them. Note that this often requires that the person you are encouraging is in the midst of their own difficult season and is looking for that sort of connection; otherwise, sharing it randomly without invitation might make things uncomfortable.

If that is the case, simply save that level of encouragement for a rainy day, and put into practice specific and believable encouragement. Praise your encouragee with authentic words.

For example, "Terrance, you are an unbelievably thoughtful neighbor. I've seen you go out of your way to help our older neighbors, shoveling their driveways, mowing their lawns. This neighborhood is definitely better with you in it!"

This message of authentic encouragement sounds much more specific and believable than "Terrance, you are a great neighbor."

I think you get the idea; it is a pretty simple principle. Bonus points if you go specific and believable using the art of "who over do" and focus on innate characteristics rather than specific skills!

The Art of Authentic Encouragement

Putting Art into Application

Learn from my lesson with Bob. When you reach out to others to encourage them, make sure you say something specific and believable. Stick to what you know about them. Remember that if you don't know someone well enough to encourage them immediately with praise, you can practice the art of care and ask them deep, meaningful questions about their lives, their hopes, and their aspirations—like you learned to do with the second question in the Art of Serving Encouragement—and you'll encourage them naturally by showing that you are interested in their well-being.

Perhaps as you practice the art of care, they'll open up, and share with you something difficult they are walking through. This will give you the chance to practice the Art of Uplifting Encouragement, helping give them some hope to hang onto during a dark season. Maybe that will be a perfect time for you to be vulnerable with them, and open up about your own challenging moments, encouraging them through the art of authenticity. Perhaps out of that, you can share some ways that you practiced the Art of Self-Encouragement in your own life, and you can help them set up their own "war room" of encouragement. Over the next few weeks, you can continue to check in with them, see how they are doing, and implement the art of consistency.

I hope you see now both the subtle nuances and the deep connections between the various practices of the Art of Encouragement. Each one has their place, but they all work together synergistically to help the encourager give the best encouragement they have to offer.

I truly believe—in fact, I *know*—that encouragement can change lives. The stories I have shared in this book are just a few examples from my life, and I invite you to reflect on your own journey and find the ways that artful encouragement from loved ones around you changed your life for the better.

In a world that actively seeks to tear us down, let's learn to build one another up in love.

Thank you for taking the time to learn the Art of Encouragement. I look forward to experiencing the better world that you help create.

Afterword

W hy do I feel so strongly about encouragement?

Is it because encouragement drives performance? Well, that is certainly part of it. Encouragement moves the needle. Trying to drive performance without proper encouragement is like being 10 flights of stairs right below the ceiling of your potential.

But that is definitely not the only reason for this book.

The real reason is because encouragement is life changing. And encouragement, lifting others up, is how Jesus has called us to live.

He calls us to see the good in people, even to love and forgive those who sin against us. Some of the most important people in the Bible made huge mistakes, but Jesus still saw their potential and used them for good.

And that is how I want to see the world.

Everyone has great potential; they just need others to believe in them. And when it comes to the world, I believe God has called us all to love, to encourage, and to make an impact through basic acts of praise and love. And as simple as it may sound, it's in that simplicity that I've found my own message, and my own direction.

I think my biggest impact as a business owner and coach is in how I encourage and call others to encourage, too. When we love each other, when we show up for each other, it makes an impact, it changes people's lives, and it spreads love.

So, I challenge you to broaden your impact with encouragement. Don't wait.

It is too important.

As I conclude this book, I've reflected on the many pages worth of personal stories and anecdotes, and I am reminded that there are certain moments in this book that point to a weakness, insecurity, or mistake from my past. Oddly, the stories of my shortcomings weren't as difficult to write about as I originally thought. In fact, it was meaningful to reflect on God's grace and goodness. It was also very meaningful to reflect on the many people who have helped me and who have shown great kindness to me on life's journey. While it wasn't as daunting as I suspected to share the shortcomings, it was still easier to pen the warm, feel-good stories, the ones where I don't look quite as bad.

My personal belief is that God wants us to share the shortcomings. The scripture says that "His power is made perfect in our weakness" (2 Corinthians 12:9). He doesn't get the same type of glory when we speak about how much we have accomplished and how great we are. At the end of the day, I want to encourage others. Beyond that, I want to share the love of Jesus. His love is the most encouraging force for good that I have ever known. As I sat down to write this book about the topic of encouragement, I felt Him saying "be you." That was the message. Tell your story. Be sincere. Aim to help.

I have poured my heart and soul into this book. My hope is that in reading it, you will be reminded that you have everything you need to be a masterful encourager of people. You don't need a platform or any special ability. You don't need to be experienced or have all the right words. You don't need a plan and you don't need a strategy. You do, however, need to be you!

Observations

To help you put into action the information you learn in each chapter, we have created a fun and meaningful challenge that we think you will find to be an impactful opportunity. At the end of Chapter 1, you are asked to write down the names of 10 individuals in your life, whether it's a coworker, your spouse, a family member, a friend, your mailman, or the check-out person at the grocery store. For the next 21 days (or however long it takes you to read this book), you are going to actively work to encourage these individuals using each of the principles you learn in this book. Each subsequent chapter has its own unique exercise to try out. As you complete each chapter challenge, write down your observations in the pages provided here!

Chapter 1 Observations

135

Observations

Chapter 2 Observations

_____

_____

_____

_____

_____

_____

_____

_____

_____

_____

_____

_____

_____

_____

_____

_____

_____

_____

_____

_____

_____

_____

_____

_____

_____

_____

_____

_____

_____

_____

_____

_____

Observations

Chapter 3 Observations

_____

_____

_____

_____

_____

_____

_____

_____

_____

_____

_____

_____

_____

139

Observations

Chapter 4 Observations

_____

_____

_____

_____

_____

_____

_____

_____

_____

_____

_____

_____

_____

_____

141

Observations

Chapter 5 Observations

Observations

Chapter 6 Observations

_____

_____

_____

_____

_____

_____

_____

_____

_____

_____

_____

_____

_____

145

Chapter 7 Observations

Observations

Chapter 8 Observations

_____

_____

_____

_____

_____

_____

_____

_____

_____

_____

_____

_____

_____

_____

_____

Observations

Chapter 9 Observations

_____

_____

_____

_____

_____

_____

_____

_____

_____

_____

_____

_____

_____

_____

_____

_____

_____

_____

_____

_____

_____

_____

_____

_____

_____

_____

_____

_____

_____

151

Observations

Chapter 10 Observations

153

Observations

About the Author

Jordan Montgomery is the cofounder of Montgomery Companies alongside his wife Ashley. From small town Iowa to a dominant force in the performance coaching industry, Jordan is a highly regarded performance coach and keynote speaker whose clients include business executives, sales organizations, athletes, and entrepreneurs.

In addition to his work speaking and coaching, Jordan is an accomplished business leader who has managed top-performing sales teams in the financial services industry.

Jordan resides in Tiffin, Iowa, with his wife, Ashley, his son, Mackoy, and his three daughters, Audrey, Claire, and Olivia.

Index

encouraging your, 85–7
God as, 56
with a heart, 64–6
recognition/praise offered by,
    38–41 (*see also specific
    types of encouragement*)
words vs. actions of, 62
leadership
    biggest myth in, 84–5
    servant, 34–5, 99–100 (*see also
        serving encouragement*)
    as transfer of energy and
        belief, 79
leading up, with illuminating
    encouragement, 85–7
Leak, Ryan, 96
Lencioni, Pat
    on leader as Chief Reminding
        Officer, 50–1
    as mentor, 96
    on personal economics, 106
    on servant leadership, 99
Life Church, 58
listening, for what is important to
    others, 67–8
Lomenick, Brad, 96–7
love
    of friends that matter, 48
    giving out of, 110
    from God, 55–6
    showing, 65
    as time given, 109
    see also caring encouragement
Love Church, 106, 107

Love Does (Goff), 65
Luke 12:6–7, 55

Mandela, Nelson, 99
marketing, 93
Matthew 6:25–33, 56
Matthew 20:26, 105
Matthew 23:11–12, 105
Maxwell, John C., 100
    on being authentic, 74
    on valuing others, 84
Maxwell Leadership
    enterprises, 100
McCormick, Lauren, 59
mental game, 27
    see also self-encouragement
Molitor, Joel, 59
Montgomery, Ashley, 59–61, 63–4
Montgomery, Audrey, 111–12
Mother Teresa, 99
Mullikin, Dale, 109–10
Murdock, Mike, 49–50
Mylett, Ed, 27

natural elevators, 94–7
natural leaders, 78–9, 88
negative thoughts, 25–6
negativity of the world, 83
neuroplasticity, 25–6
non-verbal communication, 72–3
    see also energetic
        encouragement
Northwestern Mutual Indiana, 63
Nurse, David, 94–7

O'Connell, Mike, 106–8
onboarding exercise, 3–4
over-communicating
    encouragement, 50–1

path forward, showing *see*
    vision casting
persistence, 47–8
personal economics,
    106, 108
positive thoughts, 25, 26
positive vibe/attitude, 70
    see also energetic
        encouragement
possibilities
    living in the land of, 82 (*see*
        also vision casting)
    shining a spotlight on, 87
        (*see also* illuminating
        encouragement)
power
    of actions, 61–4
    of consistent encouragement,
        49–50
    of elevating encouragement,
        91–4
    of self-encouragement, 26
    of uplifting encouragement,
        14–17
    of your words, 25–6
present, being, 73
prioritizing the *who* over
    the *do,* 38–43

see also character
    encouragement
promoting others, 92–3
see also elevating
    encouragement
Proverbs 3:3, 25
Psalm 34:18, 16
Psalm 37:23, 55
Psalm 91, 24
public recognition/praise *see*
    elevating encouragement

relational currency, 43
relational needs, 91
repeated thoughts, 26

Scherff, Brandon, 32–8
scriptures
    about God's loving care, 55–6
    counteracting negative
        thoughts with, 26
    encouragement from, 23–5
    see also specific scriptures
2 Corinthians 12:9, 130
self, dying to, 108
self-encouragement, 21–30
    being intentional about, 28
    challenge for, 27–30
    personal story of, 21–5
    and power of your
        words, 25–6
selfless care, 55–6
    see also caring encouragement